"AN...
SHA...

◊ The little boy dying of cancer who was sent back from heaven with his cure.

◊ The dying boy who met the brother his mother had never told him about on the other side.

◊ The child inspired to become a brilliant artist by the blazing lights and colors of a near-death experience.

◊ The child, condemned by doctors to death, returned to perfect health by a spirit who told him his time had not yet come.

◊ The little girl who came back from death with uncanny powers she had not previously possessed.

◊ The tiny tot who looked down at his own pale corpse and then re-entered it to bring it back to life.

◊ The child who did not want to leave heaven until an angel told him why he had to.

Let these and all the other wondrous children in this astounding book take you through the veil of darkness to the dazzling light.

CHILDREN OF THE LIGHT

CHILDREN OF THE LIGHT

The Startling and Inspiring
Truth About Children's
Near-Death Experiences and
How They Illumine the Beyond

*Brad Steiger and
Sherry Hansen Steiger*

A SIGNET BOOK

SIGNET
Published by the Penguin Group
Penguin Books USA Inc., 375 Hudson Street,
New York, New York 10014, U.S.A.
Penguin Books Ltd, 27 Wrights Lane,
London W8 5TZ, England
Penguin Books Australia Ltd, Ringwood,
Victoria, Australia
Penguin Books Canada Ltd, 10 Alcorn Avenue,
Toronto, Ontario, Canada M4V 3B2
Penguin Books (N.Z.) Ltd, 182-190 Wairau Road,
Auckland 10, New Zealand

Penguin Books Ltd, Registered Offices:
Harmondsworth, Middlesex, England

First published by Signet, an imprint of Dutton Signet,
a division of Penguin Books USA Inc.

First Printing, September, 1995
10 9 8 7 6 5 4 3 2 1

Contents

· 1 ·

Heaven Is My Home

Both of the authors survived a near-death experience (NDE) when they were children. First we will share details of Brad's journey to the other side; then, later in the book, we will describe Sherry's near-death experience.

Brad's favorite hymn as a child was "Heaven Is My Home." Somehow the opening words of the hymn's first stanza always had a special meaning to him, as if they were a reminder of a truth dimly remembered but never to be forgotten:

> *I'm but a stranger here;*
> *Heaven is my home.*
>
> * * *

On August 23, 1947, when he was a boy of eleven, it seemed as though Brad was about to return home to heaven much earlier than he had anticipated. It was on that day—his parents' wedding anniversary—that he died—or, for a time, seemed to die—as a result of a terrible accident on his family's farm in Iowa.

His body lay crushed and bleeding, sprawled where the mangling, metallic blades of the farm machinery had dropped it. Almost at once Brad's essence, his Essential Self, left his body and distanced itself from the tragic scene. Although he could clearly perceive the events taking place below him, he felt only dimly associated with the dying farm boy lying in the hay stubble and his seven-year-old sister running for help.

Brad had *become* his essence—an orange-colored spheroid, intent only on soaring toward an incredibly beautiful and brilliant light higher above him.

He felt blissfully euphoric, and he began to glory in a marvelous sense of oneness with All-That-Is.

In his book *One with the Light* Brad describes his childhood near-death experience in detail, and he writes of the phenomenon of bilocation as a facet and function of his spirit body.

> . . . I discovered a most remarkable thing: I could be in two places at once. I could exist physically in my father's arms as he carried my terribly injured body from the field; and at

the same time, I could be above us, watching the whole scene as if I were a detached observer.

When I became concerned about my mother's reaction to my dreadful accident, I made an even more incredible discovery: The Real Me could be *anywhere* that I wished to be. My spirit, my soul, was free of the physical limitations of the human definitions of time and space. I had but to think of my mother, and there I was beside her. . . . I put the newly found freedom to other tests. . . . Instantly I was beside each of [my friends] as they worked with their father on their own farms.

From time to time Brad would feel a fleeting pinch of regret over leaving his family and his friends, but whenever sorrow over earthly separation impinged on his extended consciousness, he would be shown *something* that he can best describe as a series of brilliant geometric designs. It was as if these colorful patterns were somehow a part of the great tapestry of life. It was as though the very perception of these geometric figures by Brad's elevated awareness somehow demonstrated in a very dramatic way the order and the rightness of existence.

To view this cosmic panorama was somehow to peek into God's notebook and to see that there truly was meaning to existence on Earth. There was, indeed, a divine plan. Life on Earth was not simply the result of some cosmic accident.

For many years after his near-death episode, Brad assumed that his viewing of the geometric designs had to be classified as an ineffable experience, impossible to translate into physical expression. Whenever he attempted to articulate the cosmic panorama and describe the geometric patterns for others, his mind would literally blank out for lack of an appropriate vocabulary.

In *One with the Light,* Brad stated how he finally saw images that very closely approximated what he had been shown during his NDE when, in 1988, his wife, Sherry Hansen Steiger, began to conduct healing seminars utilizing computer-derived images of fractal geometry.

Brad remembered that the geometric designs completely removed his fear of death and allowed his spirit essence to move closer to the light.

At the same time, he stated, the very light itself seemed to be intelligent and to manifest a kind of benevolent presence that brought with it peace and tranquility.

The mangled eleven-year-old Iowa farm boy was in and out of his body during a desperate 140-mile run to a hospital in Des Moines where their family doctor thought his life might be saved.

"Whenever the Real Me would enter the body of the dying eleven-year-old boy," Brad said, "it seemed to reject the choice and return to the dimension of reality where there was no pain."

Rather inconveniently, he returned to his physical body just as the surgeons were preparing to operate—and he came back with such force that he sat up, shouted, and pushed an intern off balance. It took the calming tones of love and caring from a Roman Catholic nun to pacify him until the anesthesia could take deeper effect.

I now sensed a kind of intelligence or personality within the light itself, and I asked if I might leave the operating room. I was just bobbing around above my body, and I really didn't want to watch the surgery. The accident with the farm machinery had essentially scalped me and given me numerous skull fractures. In answer to my prayer, I remember being taken to what appeared to be a kind of ideal little village, complete with bandstand, ice cream vendors, and friendly people walking about.

During the two weeks of Brad's hospital stay, the nuns seemed to have sensed that he had been "somewhere" and had seen "something," and they asked him again and again about his experience as a spirit essence, traveling between the two worlds.

A mystery had been pierced, they told him. He would never again have to ask the troubling question about whether humankind survived the experience of physical death. He would be able to testify that there was truly an existence that transcended the material realm.

Because of what could well have been a fatal accident, Brad was given to understand that we do survive physical death in our spiritual essence, our souls.

"I knew with an unshakable certainty that we are spiritual beings. Regardless of the technology that may surround us, in spite of the physical environment that may complement or discourage us, apart from political or cultural boundaries, we are spirits inhabiting a physical body—and it is the things of the spirit world that are the most lasting."

Brad has always stressed that he has never felt "chosen" or "special" because he survived near-death and was shown the cosmic geometric visions. But he has regarded himself as having been blessed with being permitted to *know* what so many others must accept by faith alone.

And because of his having received personal proof of an after-life existence, Brad is convinced that he is to testify to others that the human spirit is eternal and that we are not alone in the cosmic scheme of things. There exist benevolent beings of light to help us and to guide us in our spiritual evolution.

"My mission is to tell others of these eternal verities, to be always what my adoptive Seneca tribal name, *Hat-yas-swass*, represents: "He Who Testifies.""

Rather early on in his adolescence, Brad began more and more to perceive life as a spiritual quest.

"I came to believe that humankind is meant to strive toward a meaningful goal through a series of progressive experimental or testing episodes, each of which will contain a number of messages and/or hidden teachings that must be deciphered and understood before we may proceed on to the next sequence of life experiences."

Because of the severity of his accident, Brad was forced for quite a lengthy period of time to withdraw from all strenuous physical activities, including all contact sports.

"This was a heartbreaker for both my father and me. He was a superb athlete with a trunk full of trophies and medals. He had begun working out with me almost as soon as I was able to stand erect. Almost every night after field work and barn chores, we would train at one sport or another. Even after the doctors declared me well enough to participate, the coaches were too afraid to accept responsibility for any possible injury that I might receive to my skull. I couldn't blame them, but I felt hurt and rejected just the same."

Through the encouragement of his parents and his paternal grandmother, who was the town librarian and a tireless advocate of reading and higher education, Brad directed his attention to the world of books. He made the acquaintance of Hawthorne and Melville, Poe, and Whitman, Jack

London and Stephen Crane, Mark Twain and Ambrose Bierce.

He studied works on magic and became an amateur magician.

He found books on the paranormal, theology, metaphysics; and he was pleased to find kindred souls who were proud to be seekers and not merely ciphers.

And, later, in forays to larger cities, he discovered *Fate* magazine, a marvelous little journal of the strange, the unusual, and the unknown; and he learned that others had undergone astral journeys out of their bodies during violent accidents or terrible illnesses.

He was led to seek out the works of such psychic researchers as Hereward Carrington, Sylvan Muldoon, and Dr. Robert Crookall, who identified the kind of occurrence that Brad had undergone as a "pseudo-death experience."

After many late-night hours with the works of Emerson and Thoreau and their New England Transcendentalism; Dostoevsky, Kierkegaard, and Sartre and their Existentialism; William James, Ivar Lissner, Johann Wolfgang von Goethe, Marcus Bach, and Thomas á Kempis and their theological explorations and visionary experiences, Brad expressed his mission, born of a childhood near-death experience, in a statement of belief, a personal creed:

I believe that humankind's one truly essential factor is its spirituality. The artificial concepts to which humankind has given the designation of sciences are no truer than dreams, visions, and inspirations. The quest for absolute proof or objective truth may always be meaningless and unattainable when it seeks to define and to limit our souls.

I believe the soul is eternal, evolving higher in spiritual vibrations, seeking to return to the source from whence it came.

I believe there is a supreme being, timeless and universal, to whom all men and women may reach out and receive strength.

I believe that humankind is part of a larger community of intelligences, a complex hierarchy of powers and principalities, a potentially rich kingdom of interrelated species—both physical and nonphysical. Among these intelligences are angels, multidimensional beings, who care about our spiritual evolution.

I believe that technology plays a far smaller role in the lives of nations than the spirit, for the essence of each of us is our intellect and our soul. Machines, associations, political parties, and trade balances are but transitory realities that must ultimately wither, decay, and come to nothing. The only lasting truths are soul, imagination, and inspiration.

* * *

I believe that each man and each woman, in moments of quiet meditation, may learn to enter the silence, enrich the soul, and achieve a spiritual link-up with the blessed harmony that governs the universe.

Childhood Survivors Tell of Their Near-Death Experiences

Because of our personal interest in the near-death experience of children, we often lecture on the subject in our seminars and workshops. Questions related to childhood NDEs have always been a part of the questionnaire that we devised in 1968 to probe the expression of the mystical in the lives of ordinary people.

Of the nearly thirty thousand respondents to the Steiger Questionnaire of Mystical, Paranormal, and UFO Experiences, sixty-four percent stated that they had undergone a near-death experience—most, eighty-two percent, before the age of twelve.

Some of our respondents claim that the connection that they made with an angelic or spiritual guide during their near-death experience stayed with them throughout their childhood and into their adult life as well.

Thomas, a professional artist, remembered that when he was ten years old, he lay in a coma for three days following an automobile accident.

"While my parents prayed for me to regain consciousness and the doctors and nurses fought for my recovery, I was safe in the company of majestic figures in lavender robes and hoods who had kind and gentle eyes. From time to time I would check in on my body in the hospital room below. When it was time for me to return to my body, the beings told me that I would always be special to them and that they would be nearby if I needed them."

Once when he was fifteen and undergoing severe depression, the entities in the lavender robes appeared when Thomas was looking up at the night sky.

"They told me that I would always have a home with them in heaven. They also counseled me not to be disheartened. I would soon discover that I possessed special talents that I had not yet begun to use. Not long thereafter, I began to excel in painting and woodcarving."

According to Thomas, the lavender figures have continued to appear on occasion during his adult years, especially when he is troubled.

* * *

When Bonnie, a high school guidance counselor, was about the age of eleven, she went into a four-week comatose state as the result of an injection of antibiotics.

"I awakened very much aware that the Real Me had spent those four weeks in some realm other than the physical. I also knew that I had received many valuable spiritual teachings from angelic and multidimensional beings."

Through meditation, when Bonnie was seventeen, she established a rapport with an entity that she was convinced was one of the angels who had tutored her during her four-week sojourn in the non-physical dimension.

"I now receive regular messages from this angelic being, and I am given information that is of vital use to me on a personal level. I am also given guidance in direction in my work as a counselor to young people. The entity appears, through my 'inner' eyes, to be of human form."

At the age of eleven, Esther, a professional photographer, nearly died from a massive ear infection.

"My doctor gave up after two weeks of treatment and turned me over to a specialist on Easter Sunday. I underwent surgery and experienced unbearable pain. Because of this I am much more aware of the pain suffered by others, and I learned to respect all life—animals and insects as well as people."

Esther also received a firm link-up with her guardian angel during her near-death experience, and she has maintained an open line of communication well into her adult years.

"My angel communicates with me when I call upon it and answers questions about my personal dilemmas.

"If I am in danger, I will hear a warning. Then, in a few minutes, I will learn what the danger is.

"This angelic entity is faceless and androgynous and appears primarily as a light form."

When Lorraine, a college professor, was eleven, she was "visited" by an angel just as she was coming down with polio.

"That was before the serum had been invented. This tall, magnificent angel came to my bedside and told me that he would be with me and never leave my side.

"Although I became deathly ill and my parents thought for a while that they had lost me, I came through the sickness with no paralysis and no aftereffects at all."

Lorraine said that later, during her recovery, she was unable to see her protective angel, but she could hear his footsteps coming and going. "I could still 'feel' his presence even though I could no longer see him."

Her contact at age eleven initiated a relationship that Lorraine said has continued into her early sixties.

"During my meditations I consciously come into contact with an angel in a white robe, whom I recognized long ago as the same benevolent being that visited me when I was a child. In a light trance state—and sometimes in dreams—this entity takes me past the boundaries of our universe and into the presence of the supreme being, whose majesty I cannot describe."

Other childhood survivors of the near-death experience feel that they were given a special mission to perform when they were restored to health.

Jean, a psychiatric social worker, was only five when she recovered from a severe case of food poisoning.

"I remember that a beautifully robed entity, who, at the time, I believed to be Jesus, told me that I was being sent back to my mother and father because I had to perform a special mission of helping people. I was told that I would be guided throughout my life."

Lois was a child of ten when she was given a veritable death sentence.

"Coldly, in front of my parents and me, the doctor said that I was very ill and was not likely to live.

"That night as I lay in the hospital with a half dozen or more tubes in my arms, down my throat, and up my nose, I thought that I had died when I was visited by four Light Beings. Because I was a very religious little girl, I expected to be lifted up to heaven and taken to St. Peter at the pearly gates. Instead, the beings told me that I was, indeed, very ill. But although my illness was fatal, they would work together and see to it that I would not die. They assured me that I had a specific mission to accomplish on Earth and that I would not die until I had performed certain tasks."

Today as an adult of twenty-nine, Lois does have two chronic illnesses—but she is still very much alive. She is a teacher of "special children" and has been active in conducting special Olympics for the handicapped.

"Whenever I'm not feeling particularly well, I am met in my sleep by these same four Light Beings, who perform some kind of vibrational energy adjustments on me. Sometimes these seem to take place in an out-of-body experience.

"There is no question in my mind that these Light Beings remain emphatic about the job that I am doing with these kids. I guess both the Light Beings and the children that I work with are an integral part of my destiny."

Wallace, a poet and musician, nearly died of pneumonia when he was nine.

"I will always remember that just before I started getting better, I clearly saw this angel, who scolded me for having played in the mud on a wet and cold day.

"Around the age of eleven, I had a vision of this same angel. I remember that she used really big words that I could not understand, but I was able to remember them until I could. The essence of what she said was that I was to grow up to become aware of the world of spirit and to help others to understand that we survive physical death."

Debra, a psychic counselor, told us that angels permitted her to return to life from her NDE with the stipulation that she find others like herself who might need help adjusting to any aftereffects experienced by their having survived a near-death encounter.

"I was seventeen when I nearly died from suffocation in a fire. My mission from the angels was to locate any kids—especially young ones—who had survived a NDE and help them understand that they were not alone and that the things that they had seen and experienced did not make them weird or strange."

Debra became so gratified with the task the angels had assigned her—and she received such a sense of well-being from assisting others to understand the true meaning of their experience—that she still conducts a support group for young NDE survivors as a forty-two-year-old housewife, mother, and psychic counselor.

During a near-death experience when she was fifteen, Patricia, who has her own radio show on spiritual matters, was told that she must return to the world to help spread the true message of God.

"I returned to my body with a purpose. That is when I joined the Sisters of the Poor. But after many days of praying and meditating upon God, I realized that my heart was not content to remain. I asked permission to leave.

"I went back to the world, but I decided not to return to school. From that time on, my school was what my angelic guide taught me."

Patricia stated that she has been taken on a number of out-of-body journeys by her guide.

"Each time the guide who came to me as a child is with me. Each time I return from one of these voyages, I know that my spiritual being is very different. Each time my soul wants more and more to help humankind."

In addition to a special mission, other children are bequeathed unique talents and insights.

When Cherryl, a gifted psychic-sensitive, was eleven, she had a near-death experience that was so impressive that it left her with no further doubt that "a person does exist and have a personality-intelligence apart from the physical body." Such an assurance gave her great comfort in her teenage years, when she began a direct-voice contact that has remained an integral part of her life from that time onward.

Cherryl has received many types of messages.

"My spirit guides provide messages of guidance and warnings of danger. There is advice relating to healing myself and others. The most wonderful messages are those containing teachings of spiritual-cosmic truths."

Most recently, Cherryl said, she has been receiving messages concerning Earth changes during a period that she describes as a forthcoming time of transition for the planet.

"Some of my guides appear as white lights. Others as softly glowing golden lights. Some entities are dressed in white, monklike robes. Still others appear as kind of 'super mortals,' tall and beautiful of face and form. These graceful, perfectly proportioned beings have a slight, golden complexion, somewhat akin to a light suntan. Their green or gray eyes are almond-shaped, slightly tilted, and set over rather high cheekbones. They are most beautiful."

Arthur, a child psychologist, met an angel with a beard when, as a child of ten, he nearly drowned in his uncle's swimming pool.

"The angel told me that I would be a leader later in life. The being was enveloped in a brilliant light—or standing in front of a bright light—and he told me that I must not go beyond the light."

Arthur recalled that he was a painfully shy and awkward fourteen-year-old when he was sent by his parents to visit relatives in Miami.

"The bearded angel appeared to me one night

and told me that I could play the guitar and sing. I had never before done either one, but the next afternoon I picked up my young cousin's guitar and found out to my amazement that the angel was right! My cousin had been getting nowhere with his lessons, so I became the most popular kid in the neighborhood for the month that I stayed in Miami."

When he was sixteen, Arthur came home from school to find his father dead in the bedroom.

"I grieved for the loss of my father, but my own near-death experience had taught me that we must accept death as a transcendence to spiritual life."

At the age of seventeen, Arthur had a premonition that his older brother would be killed in an automobile accident.

"I was prepared for his death because of my established faith in God, the reality of the afterlife, and ministering angels. I saw my brother's spirit the night of his death, and I talked with him and helped him cross over into the care of his angels."

Now thirty-eight, Arthur stated in his report that he had experienced a number of accurate predictions that he had first received in dreams or visions.

There are other survivors of NDE who may not be provided with remarkable talents, but who return blessed with a sense of the indomitable power of the human spirit.

* * *

When he was eight, John, a high school teacher, was involved in a serious automobile accident that placed him in the hospital for two months.

"My father hit an oil slick on the highway on a very rainy day. He tried his best to control our vehicle, but we slammed into an embankment.

"Instantly, I was out of my body, watching other cars skid and slide to avoid hitting us. I could see my dad lying slumped against the steering wheel, but I had a sense that he would be all right."

John remembered floating through what he perceived to be "a big, black, empty warehouse" until he came upon a Light Being.

"The light emanating from this entity was so bright that I remember putting up my hands to shield my eyes. After I had just floated around the being for a while, it reached out and took my hand.

"Everything was a blur of brilliant colors after that. And then everything went completely black."

John woke up in a body cast and in a lot of pain.

"I could just tell by the way that everyone acted that nobody thought I was going to make it. I could see it in their eyes. I could tell by the way the nurses never really looked at me, and it seemed like Mom and Dad were always about to cry.

"But I knew that God had sent me back for a good reason. Later, after three operations, no one, not even the doctors, could believe how quickly I healed."

John has not claimed to have had any kind of continued contact with the Light Being that took his hand and brought him back to his body, but he wrote that he continued to be "a positive thinker with a lot of determination."

While it is true that many children describe angels, Light Beings, and other spiritual entities accompanying them through their NDE, others hear only an unseen voice guiding them through the experience or helping them to make crucial decisions of the utmost importance to their ultimate destiny.

Dorothy, a journalist, was only thirteen when she began suffering from severe depression and a wide variety of physical disorders, including colitis, gastritis, sinusitis, anemia, insomnia, bronchitis, and circulatory problems.

"One night as I lay in my bed, I found to my horror that I simply could not breathe. I tried to reach for my inhaler on the nightstand, but I must have blacked out.

"I don't really know what happened next, but I became aware of myself as a kind of orange-colored balloon floating up near the ceiling. I could look down on my body on the bed and observe it thrashing about, still trying to force air into its lungs. I really felt strangely unattached to that poor, wretched thing below, who was quite obviously dying. I actually felt relieved that my multitudinally afflicted body was dying. I felt a lot better as a balloon than as a lump of flesh beset with a dozen miseries."

While she was enjoying her newfound freedom from pain and suffering, Dorothy suddenly heard a very authoritative voice asking her an extremely important question.

"I saw no one, but I distinctly heard this deep, in-charge kind of voice ask me if I wanted to live or die. I was stunned. I mean, this freedom away from my miserable body was terrific, but was I really ready to leave my friends, my parents, my school? As lousy as life could be, was I really ready to bail out at the tender age of thirteen? After all, there were things that I wanted to see and to do, regardless of my thousand and one physical torments.

"The voice asked the question again. It somehow reminded me of our school principal making an announcement over the loudspeaker. But what the unseen interrogator was asking was far more important than what time classes would be dismissed for Thanksgiving vacation. The authoritative voice was asking me if I wanted to dismiss my life for good. And I had a strong inner *knowing* that whatever I decided *would* happen. It was really up to me whether I wished to go on living or to die."

Dorothy called out that she wished to live.

"Suddenly I felt so filled with a pulsating illumination that I felt that I must be glowing like a light bulb. I was completely saturated with such an overwhelming vibration of love that even now, at the age of forty-two, I cannot speak of it without crying. From that moment on, I knew that I would never be alone and that I would be able to handle any suffering, pain, or adversity that might come along in my life."

And then Dorothy was back on her bed, still gasping for her next breath, trying desperately to force air into her lungs.

"It truly was as if time on the physical plane had stood still. I finally managed to grab my inhaler and blast a cloud of its life-sustaining mist into my lungs. Within the next few minutes I had once again regulated my breathing."

That next week Dorothy was diagnosed as a hypoglycemic, and she found her way at last to a nutritionist-endocrinologist who helped her on the path to restored health.

◆ 3 ◆

Defining a Pattern Profile of the NDE and Its Aftereffects

Dr. Antonino Aldo Sodaro, chief surgeon of Rome's main public hospital and a professor of surgery at Rome University, has become convinced through personal observation and research that there is life after death.

Dr. Sodaro related one incident in which a teenage boy was terribly injured in a car crash. The young man floated outside of his body and rose above the accident scene. Below him he could clearly see what appeared to be his lifeless body mangled in the twisted metal of the wrecked automobile.

Although he could see men and women working desperately to free his corpse and attend to the others involved in the accident, he was experiencing a sense of absolute calm and peace. As he drifted higher and farther away from the carnage below, he began to be attracted by a beautiful light.

As he drew closer to the heavenly illumination, he was astonished to encounter his deceased grandfather, who was accompanied by a woman who was a stranger to him.

"Go back," the two entities told him. "It is not yet your time to stay here. Go back to your life. People are waiting for you to return."

The teenager became aware of a force that seemed to be tugging him back toward Earth, but he wished to stay near the light and continue to enjoy the marvelous feelings of tranquility and love.

"Listen to me." His grandfather spoke now in a stern voice. "You must return. Surrender to the force that draws you back to life."

Reluctantly, the young man obeyed his grandfather and abandoned himself to the energy pulling him back to his body.

A few minutes later, Dr. Sodaro said, as medical personnel were resuscitating the teenager, he began to speak of having seen his deceased grandfather near a beautiful, heavenly light. But the woman in the light with Grandpapa, he added, grimacing in confusion and fighting back the pain, was a stranger to him.

Residents near the accident scene who had come out of their homes to offer help to the victims were intrigued by the injured teenager's description of the woman. Although they knew it could not be so, it sounded very much as though he was describing one of their neighbors. This, they knew, could not be. Their friend was very much alive. Perhaps the poor boy truly had encountered the spirit of his grandfather, but surely he was only babbling in his agony when he seemed to describe their neighbor lady.

But, Dr. Soldaro concluded his account, when they went to the woman's residence to inform her of the bizarre coincidence, they found her lying dead in her bed. The young man had been met at the light both by the spirit of his deceased grandfather and by the very recently departed spiritual essence of a woman in the neighborhood where he had crashed his car.

Although Brad continued to use the term "pseudo-death experience" as he explored the phenomenon in his research and in lengthy chapters in his works *World Beyond Death* (1968) and *Minds Through Space and Time* (1971), Dr. Raymond Moody's best-selling book *Life After Life* (1975) established the phrase "near-death experience" as the generally accepted term for those who return from the brink of death or after being pronounced clinically dead.

Also, by 1983, after comparing our own research

data with that accumulated by other near-death phenomenologists, we found that a general consensus had emerged regarding a pattern profile of such experiences.

- Those experiencing near-death usually see their physical bodies apart from their spiritual bodies.
- A soaring sensation, a definite out-of-body movement, is felt.
- Nearly all those experiencing near-death discover that their consciousness is free of time and space and all previous physical limitations.
- A sense of disorientation and confusion is often reported in these experiences when family, friends, medical personnel, and other humans seem unaware of their nonphysical presence.
- The sensation of moving down a tunnel toward a bright light is very frequently mentioned.
- A great number of those in near-death experiences state that they encountered an angelic being, a spirit guide, or the spirit of someone known by them to be deceased, such as a friend or a relative.
- Many report having witnessed a kind of life review of their earth-plane existence.
- A glimpse of paradise or a guided tour of heaven conducted by an angelic host is recalled by many.
- An extreme reluctance to leave this beautiful state of existence and return to their physical bodies is commonly expressed.

Citing a Gallup Poll survey conducted in 1992 that revealed that around thirteen million American adults claimed to have undergone at least one near-death experience, our friend and colleague, Dr. P.M.H. Atwater, stressed that such a figure constituted roughly one-third of those who face death in a hospital or clinical setting at any given time.

"With children, however, the figure is seventy-five percent," she said, "according to Dr. Melvin Morse, who, together with Kimberly Clark Sharp and a team of associates, conducted the first empirical study done of children's near-death experiences."

Dr. Atwater, author of *Beyond the Light: What Isn't Being Said About the Near-Death Experience,* has spent many years of field work investigating the near-death phenomenon, and according to her research, children do not seem to report negative near-death experiences.

Only adults in my research base ever reported a hell-like scenario. Children didn't.

Even newborns can have a near-death experience, remember it, and tell their parents when old enough to be proficient at language, And it's the children who speak of an animal heaven that they must pass through before they can be in the heaven where people are.

Often, children encounter in the death experience *any* sibling that died before them—

even if that sibling had been but an aborted fetus. *Future* siblings are also met.

In those cases that near-death survivors claim to have been left with aftereffects, Dr. Atwater states that her research indicates that eighty to ninety percent exhibit *physiological* changes as well as psychological. Among the most frequent aftereffects reported to Dr. Atwater are the following:

- Look and act more playful
- Skin brightens, eyes sparkle, smile more
- Substantially more or less energy
- Increased sensitivity to any form of light, especially sunlight
- Increased sensitivity to any form of sound and to noise levels
- Boredom levels decrease or increase
- Can handle stress easier; heal quicker from hurts and wounds
- Brain begins to function differently

In our own research, based on responses to the Steiger Questionnaire of Mystical, Paranormal, and UFO Experiences, we found that well over eighty-seven percent of those who claimed to have undergone a near-death experience as a child still complained of hypersensitivity to sound and light as adults.

Dr. Atwater has declared the near-death phenomenon to be a "complex dynamic that addresses a broad range of issues." Although we will be referring to her important research from time to time throughout this book, we will list a few of those complex issues that she offers:

Since . . . even newborns can accurately remember their NDEs *and* the conditions of their birth, how much more can they remember and how far back does their memory go? And how does this speak to the penchant in our country to operate on little ones without benefit of anesthesia?

Since children and adults alike meet future *and* past siblings *and* "babies to be" while on the Other Side, how does this speak to the so-called randomness of the choices we make, the consequences that follow, and whom we affect? And what does this imply about abortion and the theory that the soul enters only at birth?

Since out-of-body episodes often have components in them that are later verified—some impossibly so—what does this say about the relationship between our faculties and our brain, about our ability to be completely mobile and fully functional *without a body,* and still be in possession of all our faculties?

Since near-death survivors are *physically* changed by their experiences, as well as psychologically, what does this say about the *real* power of subjective experience?

Since the part of us that has this experience "separates" from the body to the extent that it does, is that not an indication that not only do we have a soul, we *are* a soul-resident in a manifested lifeform? If that is true, what else is true about life, about death, about soul, about purpose and mission and Source and Creation?

In the February 19, 1983, issue of *Science News*, Dietrick E. Thomsen quoted George Wald of Harvard University, winner of the 1967 Nobel Prize for physiology or medicine, declaring that there are "two major problems rooted in science but assimilable as science—consciousness and cosmology." Conceding that nothing one can do as a scientist can adequately identify the presence or absence of consciousness, Wald concluded that consciousness must therefore lie somewhere beyond the parameters of time and space.

While many contemporary scientists are uncomfortable attempting to analyze such matters, Wald has stressed his belief in the importance of attempting to place consciousness and cosmology together. Perhaps, he has theorized, rather than being a late evolutionary development, consciousness has always existed. Indeed, it may have been consciousness that formed the material universe and created life and overt forms of consciousness.

"The universe wants to be known," George Wald said. "Did the universe come about to play its role to empty benches?"

• 4 •

His Big Sister Sent Him Back Home

Doctor K. M. Dale, who practiced medicine for many years in the Pittsburgh area, told of a case in which the fever of a nine-year-old boy finally broke after nearly thirty-six hours of anxious vigil on the part of his parents and hospital personnel.

Almost as soon as he opened his eyes, at three in the morning, little Edward Cuomo began to speak of having accompanied his guardian angel to heaven.

"Papa, I saw Grandma Cuomo," he told his father. "And Auntie Rosa was there."

Joseph Cuomo leaned forward and brushed strands of damp hair off his son's forehead. "Shhh, Eddie," he said. "You need to sleep now."

The child was persistent, as if he felt some urgency in sharing his otherworldly experience with his parents. "Where's Mama? I saw Uncle Lorenzo, too."

Joseph told Eddie that his mother was sleeping in another room in the hospital. She had sat by his bedside until she had nearly collapsed.

"I went to heaven, Papa," Eddie said after he had taken a sip of water from the glass that a nurse held to his lips. "I saw so many of our family there."

Joseph smiled at Dr. Dale and shrugged his shoulders. "I guess it was the fever, right, Doc? It was the fever that made little Eddie think he saw all those dead members of our family?"

Dr. Dale remembered that he tried to put Joseph Cuomo at ease. It was apparent that for some reason he found his son's story of having encountered spirits of the dead to be personally very embarrassing.

"Who can say, Joseph?" he told him. "Little Eddie was at the point of death. We nearly lost him. If you believe in an afterlife, who can say for certain what he saw?"

"I saw angels, too, Papa," Eddie went on. "I wish Mama was here so I could tell her, too. I really saw Grandma—"

"Sure, sure," Joseph agreed, gently stroking his son's forehead. "Sure, you did."

"And Uncle Lorenzo. Mama's brother—"

"There, there, Eddie," Joseph told him. "Rest now. Sleep."

"And I saw Teresa, too. She was the one who told me that I had to go back."

"Teresa?" Joseph repeated, rocking back in his chair. "You could not have seen your sister Teresa there, Eddie. You must not say such things."

Dr. Dale knew that Teresa was the Cuomos' nineteen-year-old daughter who was away at college in Vermont.

"You could not have seen Teresa, Eddie," Joseph repeated with stern emphasis.

"I did, Papa. I saw Teresa. She was so beautiful."

Joseph Cuomo got to his feet. He stood quietly for a moment, firmly gripping the back of the chair until his knuckles stood out like white marbles.

"I cannot hear this, Doc," he appealed to Dr. Dale. "How can we get Eddie to shut up?"

"You need some sleep, man," Dr. Dale admonished him. "You haven't closed your eyes in over twenty-four hours. You go lie down. I'll give Eddie something to help him rest quietly."

Eddie began to cry. "Is Teresa going to stay in heaven with Grandma and Auntie Rosa and Uncle Lorenzo? Does that mean she won't be home at Christmas time? I don't want her to stay with them. I want her home with us!"

Joseph sat back down in the chair at Eddie's bedside and rubbed his eyes with his fingers before he spoke. "Eddie, please hear me, son. Teresa is all right. She's away at college; you know that.

She's fine. I just spoke to her two nights ago. I'll call her in the morning. She'll want to hear that you're going to be feeling better. In a day or so you can talk to her on the phone for yourself."

Eddie shook his head in sorrowful protest. "But Teresa is in heaven now with Grandma and the others. I wanted to stay with her, but she said that I had to come back to be with you and Mama."

Dr. Dale recalled that he put his hand on Joseph Cuomo's shoulder and virtually ordered him out of the child's room. "I could see how much the boy's insistence that his sister had died and gone to heaven was upsetting the man. I knew that with all the strain that he had been under, a nine-year-old boy's fevered chatter could have put him around the bend."

The amazing thing of it was, however, that little Eddie's "fevered chatter" sadly turned out to be true.

Although Joseph Cuomo had believed his daughter to be in perfect health and situated safely at school when he left his son's hospital room that evening, the next morning when he and his wife telephoned the college, they learned that Teresa had been killed in an automobile accident the night before. College officials had tried unsuccessfully to reach the Cuomos at their home to inform them of the tragic news.

"Later we learned that Teresa had died instantaneously at a few minutes before midnight, just three hours before Eddie's fever had broken and he returned to speak of his visit to heaven and of seeing his sister in the company of other of their deceased relatives," Dr. Dale said. "There was absolutely no way that Edward Cuomo could have learned of his sister's death through any of what we would term normal channels of communication. I considered this case to be most evidential of life after death. For me, personally, it caused me to completely restructure my materialistic views of life and death."

◆ 5 ◆

A Prominent NDE Researcher Shares His Childhood Experience

John W. White, one of the founders of the International Association for Near-Death Studies, calls the near-death experience a "crash course in spirituality and the human potential to expand consciousness."

White, an internationally known author, editor, and educator in the fields of consciousness research, parascience, and higher human development, has held positions as director of education for the Institute of Noetic Sciences, a research organization founded by Apollo 14 astronaut Edgar Mitchell, and as president of Alpha Logics, a school for self-directed growth in body, mind, and spirit.

"My interest in spiritual experience and the nature of consciousness has been present from early childhood," White said, "but a near-death experience at age fourteen certainly accelerated it.

"As one of the founders of the International Association for Near-Death Studies in the 1970s, I obviously have a deep and abiding interest in the subject. I've written and lectured about NDEs from a theoretical, research-oriented perspective and about the experiences of others for more than two decades. But I've never written about my own near-death experience until now.

"I chose to keep my personal life out of my writing in order to direct readers' attention to my work rather than to me," White explained. "However, after twenty-plus years of writing about altered states of consciousness and noetic studies, I've decided to become more public about myself—so I'm grateful to Brad and Sherry for the opportunity to offer this brief account for their book on the near-death experiences of children."

It was during John White's fourteenth summer that he nearly died through drowning.

"The event was completely unnoticed by anyone," he recalled. "I'd gone swimming at Mixville Pond, about a mile from my home in Cheshire, Connecticut. The pond is my town's only public swimming area, although there was no lifeguard on duty in those days [circa: 1953]. I rode my bike there one sunny afternoon and swam out to a platform that had a diving board. It was about six feet above the surface of the pond, and the board added perhaps a foot more."

Fourteen-year-old John had come to Mixville Pond by himself and had not met any friends there. The beach wasn't very crowded, and the platform was empty. A few people were sunning themselves on a nearby raft.

"Feeling the vitality of youth, I began to dive in a show-off manner. It was not that I was a great diver. I simply enjoyed the feeling of performing more than routine, simple dives as my body responded to my intention of swan dive, half-gainer, back flip, and so forth."

After a few of those warm-up dives, John decided to do what he had heard some of his buddies call a "sailor dive." Today, as an adult, John knows that there is no such thing, but somehow the prevailing adolescent wisdom at the time had declared that sailors were trained to dive headfirst with their arms next to their sides in front of them.

So he did exactly that.

"I sprang on the end of the board and sailed high in the air to enter the water headfirst at a very steep angle of descent with greater than normal speed gained through attaining more than usual height.

"It was a really stupid thing to do."

John recalled plunging through the water toward the bottom, diving deeper than usual.

"So deep, in fact, that I struck my forehead on the sandy floor of the pond. The shock of the blow passed through my body at lightning speed, and I lost normal awareness.

"I was blacked out at the bottom, unconscious."

If he had been monitored by an EEG and an EKG, John knows that some vital signs would have showed, of course. His heart continued to beat, and his brain kicked in the drowning reflex, which clamps down the breathing mechanism so water can't be inhaled into the lungs. John knows that now, looking back on the experience.

"But at the time my understanding was quite different.

"I lay unconscious on the bottom of the pond for several minutes. I'm estimating that duration on the basis of two things: First, book knowledge of how long it takes before irreversible brain damage sets in from lack of oxygen; second, from contests I held with a friend during English class when we would sneakily challenge each other to hold our breath until the second hand of the clock crept around once, twice, and for me—because I usually won—a few seconds more. At that point I would have to give up and breathe—so I know that I could hold my breath for at least two minutes."

As his body rested on the bottom of the pond, John's awareness changed from blank nothingness to a sensation of wonderful, warm tranquility and security. He had no external perception, no sensory awareness.

"I was simply floating idly, feeling more peaceful than I had ever been.

"And while that languor, that serenity pervaded me, I had the fascinating experience of seeing my life pass before my eyes, as the saying goes."

John recalled that the "life review" was not sequential, but was more like "all at once." Yet, he said, "each scene was nevertheless discreet."

In reflecting upon this remarkable parade of images of his past, he commented: "I didn't watch it, strictly speaking. I lived it. I was in it. Yet I also knew that it had all happened earlier and that I was really reviewing it. There was a strange, simultaneous subjectivity and objectivity to it."

Although a kind of "life review" is often mentioned by those who investigate such spiritual or paranormal phenomena, John told us that he did not experience all of the features of a NDE that have since come to be recognized as somewhat typical in near-death research. He did not float out of his body and go down a dark tunnel toward the Light—nor did he sense the presence of a Being of Light.

"Moreover, I didn't feel judged, nor did I feel a profound reorientation of consciousness from sin and guilt—although it was clear from the review that I'd sometimes acted with shameful self-interest. But remember: I was only fourteen. I didn't have all that much life to review."

As he drifted at ease, feeling a vague sense of satisfaction, he slowly became aware of a pounding in his ears. Then he became aware of his chest heaving, trying to breathe.

"I developed a strong sense of danger and I started to panic. No light penetrated to the bottom of the murky pond. Everything was dark, so I was quite disoriented."

Then John's hand brushed the sand, and he immediately regained a sense of direction.

"I kicked my arms and legs wildly to swim to the surface—yet amid that action I thought rather calmly, *I'm drowning*.

"There was an impossible pressure in my lungs. They swelled up, trying to take in air—but the airway-stoppage factor was still active."

He moved through the water for an "agonizing time" until at last his head broke the surface.

"I was surprised to find that I could see—but I still couldn't breathe, so powerful was that life-saving reflex.

"Neither could I cry for help. In fact, I was so traumatized that I could hardly control my arms and legs to tread water."

Somehow, John reflected, by the grace of God and a strong will to survive, he managed to remain above the water while his airway opened enough for him to begin breathing again.

The people sunning themselves on the raft had not noticed his plight, but after a few minutes John was able to swim slowly toward them.

"I hauled myself up the ladder with great difficulty and lay down to rest. After about ten minutes I felt well enough to swim to shore. Then I got on my bike and rode home."

* * *

John said that he never told anyone about the event until many years later when his writing brought him in touch with such NDE researchers as Kenneth Ring and Raymond Moody.

Why hadn't he mentioned the experience, at least to his parents?

"Strangely, it didn't seem immediately important. I'd survived. I was fourteen and full of boyhood concerns. So I sort of tucked it away in memory—where it worked like slow-acting yeast in a bowl of bread dough."

Today, as John looks back on his childhood near-death experience, he says that he is infinitely grateful for it.

"It introduced me to the power of consciousness and the hidden dimensions of human life. Since then I have experienced deeper, fuller spontaneous alterations of consciousness that have impelled me to practice more deliberate means for expanding awareness, realizing ultimate values, and maturing in character. But the seed energy of that NDE was planted and grew."

John told us that the growth of such seed energy implanted by his youthful near-death experience could be summarized by the following quote from his latest book, *The Meeting of Science and Spirit*:

There is no way to enter the Kingdom except to ascend in consciousness to the Father, to that unconditional love for all

creation which Jesus demonstrated. That is
what the Christian tradition (and, indeed, every true religion) is all about: a system of
teachings, both theory and practice, about
growth to higher consciousness. But each of
us is required to take personal responsibility
for following Jesus on that way. That is the
key to the Kingdom. Self-transcendence requires honesty, commitment, and spiritual
practice to cultivate awareness. The result of
such discipline is personal, validating experience of the fact that alteration of consciousness can lead to a radical transformation of
consciousness, traditionally called enlightenment. But this, by and large, has been lost to
the understanding of contemporary Christendom. Instead, Jesus and the Bible are
idolized, and heaven is said to be located
somewhere in outer space. Awareness of inner space—of consciousness and the need to
cultivate it—is sadly lacking. *Exoteric* Judeo-
Christianity must reawaken to the truth
preserved in its *esoteric* tradition.

For example, the original form of baptism, whole-body immersion, was limited to
adults. It apparently was an initiatory practice
in which the person, a convert who would
have been an adult prepared through study of
spiritual disciplines, was held under water to
the point of nearly drowning. This near-death
experience was likely to induce an out-of-

body projection such as many near-death experiencers report today. The baptized person would thereby directly experience resurrection—the transcendence of death, the reality of metaphysical worlds and the supremacy of Spirit. He would receive a dramatic and unmistakable demonstration of the reality of the spiritual body or celestial body of which St. Paul speaks in I Corinthians 15:40-44 (apparently referring to his own personal experience with out-of-body projection). The forms of baptism practiced today—even those involving bodily immersion—are, from the esoteric perspective, debasements of the original purpose and meaning of baptism in the Judeo-Christian tradition. (I am not implicitly advocating a return to that esoteric practice; much safer, less risky methods of inducing out-of-body projection are available today. The present symbolic use of baptism is justifiable *if* it is supplemented with the necessary understanding of its true but esoteric significance.)

• 6 •

The Power of Prayer
Restored a Dying Girl
to Life

One of the most amazing examples in our files of the power of prayer to restore a child to life and to health occurred in 1963 in Massachusetts. In this dramatic case, Charlotte Lindbergh, the wife of Dr. Phillip Lindbergh, a well-known physician in the Boston area, called upon Sylvia Matthews, the wife of a Episcopalian minister, to direct healing energies toward their stricken daughter.

Eight-year-old Lisa had been hospitalized with a virus inflammation of the brain and spinal cord. From the neck down she was paralyzed on her right side, and she was losing her fight to lower the 106 degree temperature that raged through her tiny body.

To make matters worse, the young girl was also afflicted by continual convulsions, and despite prolonged periods of sedation, the doctors were unable to control the violent spasms.

Death seemed only a few hours away when Charlotte Lindbergh telephoned Sylvia Matthews.

"Mrs. Matthews, you don't know me, but I have heard of your work with what you call 'absent healing,'" she began, trying her best to keep her tears and emotions from distorting her voice. "My child is dying. I need your help. Please, please heal our daughter!"

Sylvia Matthews' voice was calm, gentle, loving. "Only God can heal, Mrs. Lindbergh. I am only honored on occasion to serve as a channel for His wondrous gifts of healing. Do you acknowledge that it is God who heals?"

Charlotte Lindbergh readily conceded the point. "I know that it is God that heals. But I can't call Him on the telephone. And people have told me that you can . . . that you can serve as a channel for God's healing. Please help us!"

Sylvia Matthews seemed satisfied with Mrs. Lindbergh's sincerity and her genuine need. "Tell me what you wish of me and tell me where you are and where the child is located."

Charlotte Lindbergh told the healer that she stood in Lisa's hospital room with her husband, Dr. Lindbergh, and a nurse, who was trying somehow to anesthetize the patient in order to prevent further convulsions. At the time Charlotte placed the call, Lisa's seizures were occurring every three or four minutes.

"What I ask of you, Mrs. Matthews, is that you pray for our daughter's recovery," she told the healer. "She is so precious to us. We love her so much. We can't lose her. We just can't. . . ."

Charlotte could no longer contain her emotions, and she handed the receiver to her husband.

"This is Dr. Phillip Lindbergh," he said, explaining the change in speakers to Sylvia Matthews. "We ask for whatever help you can give us."

There were a few moments of silence before Sylvia asked Phillip if he were a "medical doctor" or a "Ph.D. doctor."

He explained that he was a medical doctor, a general practitioner.

"Then you, too, are a healer," Sylvia said, apparently pleased with this information.

Lindbergh felt tears welling up in his eyes. "I try to be. But I am not always successful. Not even when it is my own daughter."

Sylvia got directly to the point, perceiving that there was not a great deal of time to spare. "Do you believe in God and the power of prayer, Dr. Lindbergh?"

His fingers tightened around the receiver. "Yes, I guess I do. At least theoretically. But I guess I believe more in orthodox medicine and the scientific method."

Sylvia told him that there was nothing wrong with following conventional medicine and the laws of physical science. "As long as you don't forget to keep God in the equation and the test tube, you'll be all right."

"I beg your pardon?"

"I mean that if a doctor or a scientist is able to maintain the perspective that he, too, is but an instrument of God's will, then he or she will remember to keep God in the formula for healing."

Phillip said that he thought he understood her point.

"I'm just speaking of balance," Sylvia explained further. "Being certain that we keep our spiritual energies in balance with the physical. Are you willing to work with me in healing your daughter?"

"Of course." Dr. Lindbergh felt a slight twinge of conscience when he admitted to himself that only a few weeks ago, he would have openly scoffed at any talk of "absent healing" or the "power of prayer." And he probably wouldn't have called an Episcopal minister's wife for any medical advice, either.

As if she were able to eavesdrop on his internal monologue, Sylvia informed him that he need not feel as though he were somehow betraying his scientific medical training by employing the power of prayer to seek to save his daughter's life.

"What we are about to do is to use pure science," she said. "Pure soul science. And if God wills it, you'll see that it works."

Phillip cleared his throat and swallowed his

fears. "Then I will pray for your soul science and that it will heal Lisa."

"I need to quiet myself for just a little bit," Sylvia added. "I will begin to pray intensely for Lisa at precisely eight-thirty, one half hour from now. At exactly eight-thirty, I want you to place your right hand on your daughter's forehead. Understand?"

Phillip repeated her instructions. "And I do nothing else? Just place my hand on her forehead."

"Yes. Will you do it? Precisely at eight-thirty."

He once again promised that he would follow her directions exactly. What did he have to lose? His devotion to the principles of orthodox medicine had done nothing to alleviate his daughter's suffering or to cure her illness. Perhaps it was time to seek help from a greater power.

He sat down beside his wife to wait out the thirty minutes. Charlotte had always been more conventionally religious than he. Well, perhaps when he was younger he had been more open to the concept of a loving God. But a four-year stint as an army doctor had caused him to view life as primarily cruel and essentially chaotic. If there was a God, Phillip Lindbergh had grown inclined to believe that He had long since deserted the pernicious humans who had declared themselves the superior species on the planet and left them to their own destructive devices.

But now, with his daughter's life in the balance, why not go along with this healer? If it was true that there were no atheists in foxholes, then neither, perhaps, were there any gathered around death beds.

At precisely eight-thirty, Dr. Lindbergh rose and placed his right hand on Lisa's fevered brow.

To his astonishment, he had no sooner touched her when a relaxed sigh rose from her lips, and she fell into a deep, natural sleep.

The attending nurse, a Mrs. Ethel Martinson, stated in her report that the patient's convulsions ceased as soon as her father touched her forehead.

"I had worked with the patient for hours, seeking without success to quiet and control her seizures," Mrs. Martinson wrote. "From the moment Dr. Lindbergh placed his hand on Lisa's forehead, she began to relax—and she suffered no additional convulsions from that time on."

Charlotte Lindbergh gave prayerful thanks to God, and she called Sylvia Matthews to inform her that her absent healing appeared to have been successful. "But please keep praying!" she beseeched her.

Although Charlotte had had scarcely any rest for days, she maintained her bedside vigil that night. "The following morning Lisa was still sleeping," she said. "Her right side was no longer paralyzed; and by that afternoon life had come back into her entire body."

Three days later, Sylvia Matthews found time to visit Lisa in the hospital, and Charlotte was startled to hear her eight-year-old daughter recognize her as "the nice lady who visited me in heaven."

Sylvia sat at the child's bedside to hear more of Lisa's account, and Charlotte later stated that by this point in the series of miraculous occurrences she really should not have been surprised to hear such a declaration coming from her daughter's lips.

"Two beautiful angels were walking with me and a bunch of other children in heaven," Lisa said. "At first I was sad to leave Mommy and Daddy, but the angels were so kind and good to me and they said that my new home would be with them in Heaven. Then this nice lady came walking up to the angels and told them that they would have to let me go back. She told them that my mommy and daddy needed me so much that I must go right back with her."

Charlotte began to weep and she held her daughter's hand tightly in her own. "This nice lady, Mrs. Matthews, was right, honey. Your mommy and daddy couldn't live without you."

Then, turning to Sylvia, she asked her how such things could be.

Sylvia admitted that she had no final answers to such impenetrable mysteries. "No one really knows what great energies are released when one is praying as intensely as I was," she theorized. "Perhaps some aspect of my consciousness really did manifest in heaven to plead Lisa's case before the angels."

* * *

Ten days after the remarkable demonstration of the power of prayer to manifest healing on the body of Lisa Lindbergh, the little patient was released from the hospital and allowed to return to her home.

Two months later, by Christmas, the child was completely cured, and the grateful family enjoyed a blessed holiday.

• 7 •

Diagnosed as "Hopeless," Angels Told Bobby to Expect a Miracle

S taff physicians, interns, and nurses at a large metropolitan hospital in New York were shaken by their first glimpse of the cheerful eight-year-old boy. He was so beautiful, so full of life. But everyone on the staff knew that he had been brought to the hospital to die. The child had been carefully examined, and the results of the diagnosis were conclusive: an advanced case of cancer.

A physician we'll call Dr. Ginsberg was an intern at the time, and he has always remembered the positive outlook of both the child and his parents, Mike and Carol Owens. He had hoped that the results of the tests were somehow incorrect.

When he spotted Dr. Crane, the head resident, in the physician's lounge one morning after the child had been admitted, he asked him if the results of the examination of Bobby Owens must really be considered conclusive.

"No chance of error," Dr. Crane told Ginsberg as he handed him a set of X rays. "Bobby Owens has an advanced case of cancer in his thigh bone."

Ginsberg wanted to know the boy's chances for survival.

The head resident shrugged. "Darn slim. Assuming we can perform surgery successfully and stop the cancer from spreading, there is still the five-year survival rate with this type of cancer."

Ginsberg returned the X rays. "What does that mean?"

Dr. Crane poured fresh coffee into an oversize cup with the title SUPER DAD printed on it. "Well, Ginsberg, we know that, statistically, only about five percent of the patients with this type of cancer will be alive five years from now—even after our best efforts."

The intern winced at the low odds. "That's not so good."

Dr. Crane shook his head sadly. "It's not a pleasant statistic."

"Two days later, I learned something even more unpleasant," Dr. Ginsberg recalled. "I found out that Bobby's parents had refused to allow surgery to be performed."

At his first opportunity, Ginsberg went to the boy's room, determined to convince Mr. and Mrs. Owens to change their minds.

"I found his father, Mike, there, and I asked him to step out in the hall with me," Dr. Ginsberg told us. "I'm afraid that I was pretty full of myself in those days. I had ranked high scholastically in medical school, and I was proving myself under fire every day as an intern. Dr. Crane had gone out of his way to compliment me and to offer words of encouragement on many occasions."

Although he was quite embarrassed to admit it, he said that he began the conversation with Mike Owens by asking the man why he wanted to kill his own son.

"Talk about a warm bedside manner, eh?" He shook his head and laughed wryly at his youthful indiscretion.

Owens had narrowed his eyes and stared hard at the young doctor. "Dr. Ginsberg, I love my son. I would give my life for him. Why would you say such a terrible thing to me? I am not killing him."

Ginsberg pressed his point. "Then allow us to perform surgery. We want to save his life. We want to give him a chance to live."

Owens lowered his head and tears coursed over his cheeks. "Dr. Ginsberg," he began, then his voice broke and he took several deep breaths in an attempt to regain control of his emotions. "Dr. Ginsberg, were you on duty today?"

Ginsberg frowned, said that he'd had the previous day off and had just returned to work.

"Yesterday, Dr. Ginsberg, Mrs. Owens and I insisted on more tests being run. Somehow . . ." His voice trailed off, and he stood silently for several moments, as if summoning courage to complete his thoughts. "Somehow the cancer has now spread to both of Bobby's lungs."

"Oh, my God! I didn't know."

"That's why we denied surgery," Owens said. "Our son's time is so limited. Why subject him to any more suffering and pain than is necessary?"

Dr. Ginsberg remembered being rocked backward as if an invisible fist had punched him the chest.

"I walked away from the poor man, feeling as though I were a piece of scum two inches high," he said. "How dare I come on like that to a father who was doing his best to bear his grief with a semblance of dignity? How dare I accuse such a man of wishing to kill his son? And how dare that damn insidious cancer eat away at a beautiful child's life?"

After a lengthy discussion with Dr. Crane, Mike and Carol Owens did decide to allow Bobby to undergo radiation therapy. Shortly after the first few sessions the game little boy suffered a very high fever.

"I had been stopping by to see Bobby from time to time," Dr. Ginsberg told us, "and I never ceased marveling over his positive attitude and his cheerful personality. The little guy was really indomitable."

Bobby's miracle occurred as he was recovering from a second bout with a very high fever.

"I was just entering the room when I heard him say something to the nurse and his parents," Dr. Ginsberg said. "I will never forget the sacredness of that afternoon. It seemed as though one could sense something holy and loving had entered the hospital room."

The nurse asked Bobby to repeat what he had said.

"I'm going to get well now. The angels told me so."

"Did you have a nice dream, honey?" Carol Owens asked her son, taking his little hand in her own. "Did you dream about angels?"

"It wasn't a dream, Mommy," Bobby insisted. "I was in heaven with angels and lots of other boys and girls. And I saw Grandpa Owens there with his old dog, Zipper."

Mike Owens chuckled, leaning closer to Bobby so he would be able to hear his answer. "And how is old Zipper and Grandpa?"

"Fine," Bobby smiled. "Grandpa said to tell you not to forget to give his arrowhead collection to the pioneer museum."

Dr. Ginsberg said that he had been about to leave the boy's room, but the strange look on Mike Owens' face caused him to stay a few moments longer. Something unusual was going on in Bobby Owens' hospital room. He could sense it.

Later, he learned that Mike Owens' father had

died when Bobby was not quite four years old. Mike had promised his father before he died that he would transport his extensive collection of Native American artifacts to a friend's small museum in the senior Owens' hometown in New Hampshire, but he had never got around to making the trip. He could not recall ever having mentioned the unfulfilled promise to Bobby, and he knew of no way that the boy could have known of it.

"I'll get to go home pretty soon, Mom," Bobby said with an expansive smile. "The angels said that I would soon be all right. So did Grandpa."

Carol Owens only nodded, blinking back tears.

"No one spoke at all," Dr. Ginsberg recalled. "Who among us wished to interrupt the little boy, who was telling us about his happy dream of angels, departed dear ones, and miracle cures when we all knew that he had only a very short time to live."

Little Bobby spoke for nearly ten minutes about his having walked into a bright light and seen a beautiful angel who had taken him by the hand and led him to heaven.

"The angel told me that I was not going to heaven to stay," Bobby emphasized, "but just to rest and get all better before I came back to my hospital room. The angel said that it was not the right time for me to stay in heaven. He said that no matter what the doctors might tell me, I am going to get well!"

Incredibly, Bobby was one hundred percent correct.

"In spite of about the worst odds imaginable, Bobby Owens is now a healthy twenty-five-year-old," Dr. Ginsberg said. "Although his condition was declared hopeless on three different occasions, he has rallied each time to conquer the disease. Cancer did leave its mark on his body, however. Because the malignancy had so pervaded his left thigh bone, his leg had to be amputated."

Dr. Ginsberg went on to stress that none of the physicians who attended the unusual case are able to explain how Bobby's healing miracle was accomplished.

"Dr. Crane wrote a detailed article about the Bobby Owens case that was published in a prestigious medical journal as a possible incentive to further research by interested medical researchers. He did, however, leave out all references to angels, Heaven, and spirits of the deceased."

One physician who became intrigued by the case stated that she would have to rule out the radiation therapy as having effected the cure. "The patient did have two attacks of high fever during the therapy, but this has been noted in previous cases," she said.

Another physician who served as a consultant during the preparation of Dr. Crane's manuscript on the Owens case commented that the cure of Bobby Owens appeared to be an excellent example of "spontaneous regression of the disease of cancer."

And what, exactly, is spontaneous regression?

"That's the name we doctors put on something we do not understand," admitted Dr. Ginsberg.

• 8 •

Cured of High Fever and Allergies by a Light Being's Healing Sword

Because Larry Galwith was born with many minor to moderate orthopedic defects, his birth accelerated the disintegration of his parents' marriage and the onset of his mother's first nervous breakdown.

"I was only a couple of years old when my father left us, my mother entered an asylum, and I was given into the care of my maternal grandparents, John and Charlene Dunn," Larry stated in his report to us.

"Thank God for the sake of my own mental health that Grandmom seemed delighted to have me around. As I grew older, however, I frequently overheard Grandmom and Grandpa telling both friends and family that my mother had had no business having a child in the first place."

Unfortunately, Larry often interpreted those overheard observations as complaints or as suggestions that *he* had really had no business having been born.

"Most of the time, because of my circumstances, I felt unliked and unwanted. And when Grandmom would seek to discipline me by admonishing me that 'God didn't like little boys who were late coming home from school' or 'God didn't like little boys who didn't like broccoli and clean their plates,' I really began to believe that I was inherently unlikable. Grandpa didn't pay much attention to me at all until it was time for him to take off his belt and to spank with it, so I didn't figure that he liked me all that much, either."

Coupled with his lack of self-esteem, Larry's chronic illnesses due to his numerous allergies made him feel as though he had no redeeming qualities.

"It seemed very obvious to me that Grandmom was right about God not liking me, because He made me sick just about all the time.

"It seemed as though I was always sick and missing out on school because of sinus infections, colds, hay fever, bronchitis, and every flu bug that came down the road."

Grandpa died one night in his sleep when Larry was nine. Because he had heard him coughing earlier in the evening, the boy was stricken with guilt, thinking that his grandfather had somehow caught a bug from him and had died from its effects.

When Larry was eleven, he himself nearly died.

"I had suffered from alternating bouts of asthmatic bronchitis and viral pneumonia during most of the winter and early spring of my eleventh year. I ran high fevers, and at one point I nearly starved because Grandmom was ill at the same time—and we were both too sick to realize that I wasn't taking my medicine or eating and drinking."

It was during that period of high fever and deprivation of nourishment and medication that Larry underwent a near-death experience.

"All of a sudden one night I was up near the ceiling looking down at my fevered body below on my bed. At first I was scared out of my wits. I thought that I had died."

Larry recalled hovering over his body for what seemed to be a very long time.

"If I was dead, I began to wonder, why weren't there angels or someone to take me up to Heaven? After so long of my just bobbing around near the ceiling, I decided that I was not dead, but that the *real* me, the spirit part of me, had somehow slipped out of the body. Then I got real worried that I wouldn't be able to get back in!"

As still more time passed, Larry reconsidered his previous conclusion and decided that he really must be dead.

"Since I wasn't going to Heaven, I figured that

Hell must be bobbing for eternity up near my bedroom ceiling. Although I couldn't form words or make any kind of sound, I *felt* as if I were crying and calling out for help."

When help did arrive, Larry wasn't certain if he should have made a fuss.

"Right next to me there suddenly appeared the image of a big, strong man who was glowing in a kind of rainbow of blue, white, and violet colors. In his right hand he held something that looked like a sword.

"When he began to speak to me, the sound of his words made me vibrate. I was never able to remember all of what he said to me, but the gist of it was that I must shake off all those feelings of inferiority that had always beset me and that I must begin to reject the constant round of allergies and illnesses that had blighted my young life.

"Then he lunged at me with his sword and seemed to run me through—only it wasn't really a sword and it didn't hurt. It just kind of gave me something like an electric shock that seemed to energize me.

"The next thing I knew, I was back in my bed and feeling very, very hungry."

Larry remembered crawling to the kitchen and making himself some rice.

"Why I did that, I don't know. There was food on hand that didn't require cooking. I ate the rice with butter and sugar and milk, and I started feeling better right away."

Larry Galwith told us that he continued to receive "glimpses of similar majestic beings" sporadically until he was well into adolescence.

"There were no experiences as dramatic as being run through with Michael's healing sword," he said, revealing that in his eleven-year-old analysis of his angelic encounter he had met the archangel Michael, who had cured him of the high fever and numerous allergies. "But from time to time I would catch sight of a beautiful, majestic entity, seemingly ablaze with blue, violet, or white light."

For quite some time after his out-of-body healing experience, Larry claimed that he had rather powerful clairvoyant and precognitive abilities.

"I started to block them when I was fifteen," he said. "I had a vision of Grandmom Dunn's death, and when it came to pass as I had envisioned it, I told the angels that I didn't want to possess such an ability any longer."

Interestingly, Larry stated that he was certain that he still received occasional messages from angelic beings with whom he had somehow made a cosmic connection when he had his NDE.

"I am now nearly forty years old, but sometimes in my dreams or when I am meditating, I receive messages that I am certain come from spiritual beings. They tell me how to make my life better or how to help others who have asked for my help. There have also been times when they have shown me how I'm messing up—and what the future holds for me if I continue moving forward in the manner in which I am currently living."

◆ 9 ◆

He Saw an Angel Praying for His Recovery

It was not until Steve Cosette was nearly eighteen years old that his parents finally admitted to him that he had almost died from a severe case of scarlet fever when he was nine.

"That was when the most incredible experience of my life began to make sense to me," Steve told us. "I knew then that I must have passed some kind of crisis point the night I awakened and saw an angel praying at my bedside."

Although today he is a successful fifty-seven-year-old investment counselor who lives in a suburb of San Francisco, Steve has clear memories of his childhood in rural Oklahoma—especially the night that a merciful angel manifested to pray at his sickbed and to heal him of a terrible illness.

"At that time we lived in a tiny village in the eastern part of Oklahoma. I can remember coming home from school feeling very sick and dizzy. I think I must have been out of my head for several days before the doctor came. They still made house calls in those days. It was the mid-1940s, and penicillin was just becoming the big deal cure-all. I can remember the doc sticking a bunch of needles into various accessible sections of my anatomy, but, regretfully, the new wonder drug did not do diddle-lee-dee for me."

All Steve knew at the time was that he was very sick and nothing seemed to make him better. Much later he learned that the illness had so ravaged his nine-year-old body that the doctor had begun to prepare his parents for the worst.

"One night I awakened with clear vision and a mental alertness that I had not experienced for over a week. I looked at the big old alarm clock with the luminous dial and saw that it was midnight.

"I just lay there in the midnight stillness, and I began to wonder if I was ever going to get well. For a fleeting moment I considered that I might die, but I rejected that out of hand. I knew that my mother wouldn't let me die."

Steve remembered that he prayed to God to make him well—just as soon as He could, please.

"I started to think about God, and I got a little depressed. With the care of the entire universe on

His shoulders, how could He possibly find time to worry about me and how sick I was?

"Then I really got upset worrying about whether or not I had been too sinful for God to want to heal me. I thought about how merciless I had been to some of God's smaller creatures.

"Fancying myself both a nature lover and a scientist, I had caught lots of insects and a bunch of small fish, frogs, tadpoles, and crawfish in the creek near our home. I had placed the array of aquatic specimens in small tubs and buckets and experimented with them to see how long they could live in captivity.

"The insects I had killed by smothering them in a jar and then mounting them on pins. I had carefully placed them in neat rows in cotton-lined boxes so that I could display them at the county fair.

"Now as I lay there in the midnight stillness, I asked forgiveness if I had been ruthless and wantonly disrespectful of lower life forms.

"After all, I accused myself, were they not also an aspect of God's handiwork?

"And, in the larger perspective of God's infinite universe, couldn't some life form higher than I regard me as nothing less than a bug on which to conduct experiments?

"Perhaps I was less than an insect in God's eyes."

Steve recalled that he worked himself into such

a tearful and fearful frenzy that he was about to call out for his mother.

"I would surely have done so, but I was afraid that I might attract the ghost that I was certain lived in the attic. I was positive that such a being existed behind an old truck in the small attic area above my room. Many was the night that I was certain that I heard its footsteps stride across the attic floor and make its way down the stairs, stopping here and there to inspect various aspects of the house, then walk down into the basement.

"I lay quiet, listening for its telltale footsteps. I was weak from my long bout with scarlet fever, and I knew that I was not up to a confrontation with the attic ghost. On this night, however, I heard nothing but my father snoring in the north bedroom that my parents occupied."

Steve suddenly felt extremely weak, nauseated. His vision was once again becoming blurred. He felt as though his skull was being filled with burning sand.

"I had experienced a brief period of clarity and a respite from the debilitating illness. Now, it seemed, the sickness was returning with a vengeance."

It was at that point that Steve became slowly aware of a soft blue light at the foot of his bed.

"As I watched in astonishment, I saw the form of a beautiful angel beginning to take shape before my eyes. As the image became clearer, I saw that he—or she—was kneeling in prayer."

Steve was mesmerized as the angelic entity appeared to grow in physicality.

"The marvelous being soon appeared as solid as my bed, my dresser, myself. In the soft blue light I could see that the angel's features were very solemn, almost sad. I felt as though he must be the bearer of sad news. I became increasingly convinced that he had come to take me with him to heaven."

Panic-stricken, Steve did not know what to do.

Should he call for his parents? He didn't want to die without saying good-bye to them and telling them how much he loved them.

Should he speak to the angel? Perhaps he could ask him for more time.

And then Steve noticed that when the angel's head was not bowed in prayer, the luminous being would turn his gaze to the ceiling, as if importuning God to listen to his prayer.

"That's when I realized that the angel was praying for me to get well!"

There was a strange whirring sound, and Steve suddenly felt as though his entire body were spinning.

"Everything went totally black, and I thought I might have gone blind.

"Then I saw this bright, bright light way off in the distance. I felt myself drawn to it, and I just seemed to begin to float toward it. It was as if I was in some kind of tunnel, but I didn't have to walk to move toward the light.

"And then I heard what must have been the angel praying for me: *'Most Merciful Lord of Hosts, allow this child to continue his life on Earth. Enrich his knowledge and his understanding so that he might prove to be a better servant of thy word and thy truth. Keep him ever steadfast in the Light and keep him always from the darkness. Most Divine Lord of Heaven and Earth, remove the sickness from his body and return him anew to his full life span.'* "

Steve knows that there was much more to the angel's prayer, but he has always remembered that portion.

"All the while the angel was praying, I felt myself being slowly pulled back from the magnificent light. And then I was back on my bed."

The angel was once again becoming one with the soft blue light that Steve had first noticed at the foot of his bed.

"Just before the beautiful heavenly being disappeared, though, I saw him smile—and I knew that I was going to be all right.

"I fell into a deep sleep, and when I awakened the next morning, drenched in sweat, Mom gave thanks to God that my fever was broken. She took my temperature and said that it was normal."

The next day Steve was able to sit up and eat a bowl of vegetable beef soup and listen to the radio in the living room. The prayers of his angel intercessor had been answered.

"The next week I was back in school. My first day back in our church's Sunday school, I thought really hard about the way that angel had prayed for me to get well, and I began a practice that I have continued to this day—tithing, the spiritual discipline of returning ten percent of whatever you have to the Lord. That first Sunday my tithe was three cents. Over the years, as the Lord has seen fit to make me prosper, my weekly tithe has been considerably higher."

· 10 ·

Spirit Friends Took Him on a Tour of the Children's Heaven

Peter Fadden, a fifty-five-year-old architect from New Jersey, provided us with an astonishing account of an extremely detailed out-of-body experience that occurred to him when he nearly died of rheumatic fever as a boy of eleven.

Peter told us that he had faded into a kind of fevered reverie in which he seemed to experience a kind of life review.

"Obviously at age eleven I did not have a great deal to recall, but I began seeing snatches of outstanding birthday parties and Christmases and playing ball with my dad.

"I must have been babbling a lot of this out loud, for I can still hear the urgency in Mom's voice when she told my older sister, Jessie, to call the doctor. Dad was stationed in Korea, and Mom was really not handling the stress of my illness too well."

While Peter was in the midst of his life review, he was surprised to see two strangers walk into his bedroom.

"All of a sudden there was a nun and a priest standing at my bedside. I could see that it was not Father Murphy, our parish priest, or any of the sisters that I knew; but I was convinced that Mom had called in a priest to perform the last rites. And when I said aloud that I saw a nun and a priest standing beside my bed, Mom completely lost it.

"I remember Jessie coming back into the room and hugging Mom, trying her best to calm her, and Mom screaming, 'He's dying. My angel boy is dying!' And then everything went black for a while."

The next thing Peter can remember is waking up in what appeared to him to be some kind of hospital room.

"The thing was, though, it only had three sides; and I could look out over beautiful rolling meadows with flowers, butterflies, and grazing deer. And the room had no ceiling, so I could look up at white clouds and a bright blue sky. And then I noticed the nun and the priest standing against one of the walls."

The priest smiled and walked closer to the bed on which Peter lay. "How are you feeling, Peter?" he asked with a warm smile.

"Where am I? And who are you, Father?" Peter wanted to know.

The nun stepped forward and took his hand. "We're friends, Peter, here to help you."

"Where are Mom and Jessie? And *where is this place*?"

"Now, now," the nun tried to comfort him. "You must not get excited. Just lie still for a while and relax."

Lying still and relaxing were impossible until he got some answers. Peter sat up in bed—and that's when he noticed that his fevers, aches, and pains had vanished.

"Aha," the priest laughed. "You've noticed something very wonderful, haven't you? All those nasty aches and pains are gone. Isn't it wonderful?"

Peter had a growing sense of realization that a very dramatic change had just occurred to him.

"This—this place—"

"Isn't there a lovely view from your room?" the nun interrupted. "All the animals and flowers and birds—"

It was Peter's turn to interrupt. "The two of you were in my room. I saw you in my room back on . . ."

"Yes?" The priest nodded. "Back where?"

Peter finished his incredible thought. "Back on Earth. I've died, haven't I? And this is . . ."

"It's a kind of heaven," the nun said, completing his sentence, as if she could easily read his mind.

"And the final word has not yet been pronounced whether or not you are dead."

"But then why am I *here*?" Peter wanted to know.

The priest laughed softly, not in derision but in a kind of admission of his own inadequacies. "Neither of us can answer questions like that, Peter. We are merely messengers."

"Messengers?" Peter echoed. "You're not really a priest and a nun, are you? You're angels!"

"Just call us your friends." The nun smiled. "You may call me Maureen. And let's call him Henry."

Peter shook his head in disbelief. He still had a body that he could recognize as his own. Henry and Maureen looked like regular people. And there was a beautiful meadow spread out before him on a bright day.

"Death isn't anything like I thought it would be," he sighed. "I wasn't expecting anything like this."

Henry acknowledged his wonderment. "I don't suppose anyone really knows what to expect. Except perhaps a very few. And perhaps it is a little different for everyone."

Maureen sat beside Peter on the bed, and he noticed at once that she was no longer in a nun's habit.

"We really didn't know how to appear to you," she explained. "We knew that you were a good Roman Catholic boy, but we really thought that you might be somewhat frightened of angels with large, spreading wings and stern countenances. We were afraid that you would believe that we had come to haul you off to Purgatory or some terrible place of judgment."

Peter spoke up on his behalf. "I've tried never to misbehave terribly. And I've always gone regularly to confession."

Maureen smiled and patted his hand. "Relax, lad, we've nothing to do with judgment and punishment. We are all spirits here, and if there does exist such a place of torment, we know nothing of it—and have nothing to do with it."

Peter was somewhat relieved, but he was still puzzled by his present circumstances.

"What—what do we do now?"

Henry shrugged his shoulders. "Nothing. At least not for a while."

"Well," Peter said, pursuing the matter, "are you the welcoming committee or something?"

Maureen squeezed his hand. "It's best that you just think of us as your friends. We've been your friends, after all, for a very long time."

Henry nodded. "We've been watching over you since you were born."

"Then you *are* my guardian angels." Peter smiled, pleased with the identification.

"If you are happy with such a designation, that is fine with us." Henry smiled patiently. "We know that you humans are always more comfortable when you have given something a name."

Maureen got up from the edge of the bed where

she had been sitting beside Peter. "We could show the lad around the place a bit, eh, Henry?"

Henry nodded approval of her suggestion. "Why not? Would you like a bit of a guided tour, Peter?"

Peter hesitated. "Sure. I guess so. But not in my pajamas."

Maureen laughed. "I know you like to wear those old jeans with your plaid corduroy shirt. How about that?"

Before Peter could answer, his light blue pajamas had been replaced by the familiar jeans and plaid shirt. "They feel *real!*"

Henry clapped his hands together in merry response to Peter's astonished observation. "Of course they're real. Real, that is, for this dimension. This is a realm of mind and spirit. Thinking makes things so. A lesson, by the way, that should be always remembered on the Earth plane: Thoughts are things!"

Maureen handed Peter a bowl of fruit. "You'll find these very real, too. Help yourself to what you fancy. We brought them here especially for you."

Peter hesitated, then reached for a bright red apple nestled among bananas, plums, grapes, and pears. "Delicious," he pronounced after a tentative bite. "It tastes just like a juicy apple."

"Because that's exactly what it is, lad." Maureen chuckled at Peter's baffled revelation. "Have another, please."

"Maybe just one more," Peter said. "Won't you

have some? I hate to think of all this nice fruit going to waste."

Henry helped himself to a pear. "Nothing goes to waste here, Peter," he explained. "Everything that is unwanted or unused returns to its source."

Maureen popped a couple of grapes into her mouth. "You couldn't actually destroy anything here on this dimension however hard you tried, lad."

Henry took the bowl and held it a bit above his head. "Have we all had enough?" he asked.

When each of them indicated that this was so, Peter was amazed to see that the fruit and the bowl in Henry's hands seemed to evaporate before his eyes.

"As we were saying, lad," Maureen reminded him, "not a single thing here goes to waste. Everything that is unwanted simply fades away and returns to its source."

"And now I think that it is time for that guided tour of this level of the spirit world," Henry said.

Peter recalled being ushered across the green meadow and through a series of lovely gardens. All the colors were more brilliant, and the plants and flowers more lush and vibrant, than any that he had ever seen on Earth. In the distance he could see a beautiful golden temple from which soft, tranquil music seemed to emanate.

After a time they stood in an area in which they beheld dozens of small children at play. A number of angels or teachers had separated other groups of children and appeared to be giving them instruction in various subjects.

Maureen and Henry explained that this area was the children's nursery of heaven.

"The souls who pass over as children or who die in the process of physical birth are rejuvenated here and grow as they would have grown on the Earth plane," Maureen said.

Henry reached down to playfully tussle the hair of a small Asian boy. "Here the children of all ages are given such treatment and care as would never have been possible for them to receive on Earth."

Peter was in awe of the splendor of the place. "It is so beautiful here!"

Maureen agreed. "And with purpose. It is so designed that the young child, whose mind is not yet fully formed or contaminated by earthly influences, will find itself upon awakening in heaven in a realm of great beauty."

Peter noticed that while they stood there, multicolored shafts of light appeared to be issuing from the golden temple and were spreading their glorious illumination over all the landscape. The shafts of light seemed to be constantly on the move, interweaving themselves and creating the most vivid blendings of color, as if they were a succession of animated rainbows. The mixing of the colors produced within Peter a sensation that was both tranquilizing and vitalizing at the same time.

"No one could ever be sad or unhappy here," Peter said.

* * *

After several moments of watching the small children at play in their beautiful nursery setting, Maureen and Henry guided Peter to an area where older children resided. It was a section, Peter recalled, where there were a number of delightful ponds and small lakes.

The homes were constructed of a kind of translucent ceramic substance that resembled pearl in which a rainbow of subtle colors had been somehow incorporated into the building materials. The style of architecture very much resembled that found in various Earth cultures. The size of the individual houses had been scaled down to accommodate children of Peter's general age and dimensions.

"This area has been designed to make the child feel as much at home as possible after he makes his transition from Earth life to the heavenly sphere," Henry told him.

Peter could not help commenting that so many of the quaint little cottages looked very much like the houses found in the pages of fairy tales and children's storybooks. He asked if such a stylized architecture was also a part of the plan to make children feel at home.

"Before you go concluding that the spirit world does nothing but borrow from your Earth world," Maureen stated, "this is a good example of those instances wherein a creative person in the physical world has visited our realm during sleep or a trancelike state and been inspired by these quaint little houses in heaven."

As they continued walking, Peter's angelic friends informed him that large numbers of children lived in the tiny dwellings, each presided over by an older child who had been carefully tutored to be able to attend to any situation that arose.

Peter observed groups of happy children scattered throughout the area. Some of the children were playing games with one another; others were seated on the grass while a teacher read or lectured to them.

"I guess this would be the place—I mean if I stay, this is the place . . ."

Henry assisted him with the awkward question. "Yes, Peter, if it is decided that you are to remain here, this would be your home in the heavenly realm."

Peter agreed that it was a very pleasant place, but it was very different from his neighborhood in the New Jersey city where he lived with his family.

It was at that point that Maureen seemed to be listening to a voice inside her head.

"What is it?" Henry asked.

The expression on her face was difficult to analyze as she told her partner that Peter had to be returned to his physical body.

Henry gave Peter a playful punch on the shoulder. "It's not your time, yet, little friend. It's back to New Jersey, pain, aches, discomfort, strife—"

"And *life!*" Maureen interjected.

Henry smiled and nodded as he reached out to take Peter's hand. "Let's go!"

The last thing Peter remembered before he woke up back in his physical body was Maureen telling him that they would always be with him.

"Dr. Fogarty was with Mom and Jessie when I opened my eyes," Peter told us. "My reality was still very blurred, and I was pretty much in and out of consciousness, but I could tell that Mom was hysterical. I gave a silent prayer of thanks when I heard Dr. Fogarty tell Mom that before he left he would give her something to help her relax and to sleep."

Peter had to endure a long period of convalescence. "I was basically bedridden for three months. I didn't tell anyone about my visit to children's heaven. I knew that it was very real to me, but I knew that Mom would think that I had gone crazy with the high fever. Also, the thing of it was, a lot of what I had experienced did not fit in with my family's very conventional Catholicism; and I knew better than to ruffle any feathers in the home nest. Besides, a couple of months later, Dad was wounded in Korea and was sent home to convalesce in a veterans' hospital for nearly half a year. Mom had more than she needed to trouble herself."

According to Peter, he finally told Jessie, his older sister, when he was around seventeen and she had her own apartment in Brooklyn.

"Jess had sensed that something really weird had happened to me. She had spent hours in a bedside vigil, and she had actually kind of picked up through a sixth sense or whatever a lot of the things that were actually happening to me on some level of consciousness.

"Thankfully, she believed me, and that encouraged me to be more open in discussing my experiences with other people. I am always happy to share my story if it can help some child understand that he or she isn't crazy and that those of us who have had these kinds of experiences may have been privileged to have been given a preview of what awaits us on the other side."

· 11 ·

She Survived When Angelic Guides Spoke Through Her Comatose Body

In this most unusual case from the literature of early near-death experiences, a teenage girl survived a NDE because of the instructions that appeared to issue forth from angelic or multidimensional spirit guides that had temporarily possessed the ostensibly deceased child.

Seventeen-year-old Sarah Gunderson had always been one of those children who delighted the hearts of her elders.

If there were household chores to be done, the beautiful, blond, blue-eyed Sarah cheerfully did them. If there were children younger than she with scraped knees or wounded egos, Sarah was there to give comfort and first aid. When it was bedtime for the children, the whole family enjoyed listening to Sarah's clear, sweet voice as she sang her younger brothers to sleep with gently lullabies.

By the age of seventeen Sarah was a bright young girl with a promising future ahead of her. Her years of singing with the church choir had prompted interest from the choir director, and in the fall Sarah would be going to college with a music scholarship.

Then came the day in early July 1934 that Sarah fell ill.

Her father, Dr. Thor Gunderson, was a prominent physician in Eau Claire, Wisconsin, and he rushed to his country home as soon as the message reached him regarding Sarah's illness.

Dr. Gunderson desperately rendered what medical treatment he could, then admitted to his wife in a helpless whisper that there was nothing more that could be done for their daughter. Sorrowfully, the older children were summoned home, and the family gathered around the stricken girl's bed and began the long wait for death to arrive.

Sarah was in a coma-like sleep for many hours. Suddenly she roused herself and startled her parents by sitting bolt upright.

"Mommy, Daddy," she exclaimed, "I just saw my own funeral. I was with my guardian angels, and I looked down from heaven to watch my own funeral at Good Shepherd Church."

Dr. and Mrs. Gunderson hastily called the other children, and once the entire family had joined

Sarah in her sickroom, the teenager told them of her vision.

"I had just died," she told them, "and you were all sitting around my bed, like now, crying. Only I was outside of my body with my angels and feeling very much at peace. I felt so sad that I was unable to talk to you or to find a way to let you know that I was all right. I tried and tried, but none of you were able to hear or see me.

"Then everything got kind of fuzzy, and when it refocused, we were in Good Shepherd Church. All of our friends and relatives were there, even Aunt Mary from South Dakota.

"Pastor Jacobsen had a nice sermon and said lovely things about me. The choir sang, 'Beautiful Savior,' one of my favorite hymns, and then the congregation sang, 'This Is My Father's World.' I watched everything from heaven with my angels."

Everyone in the Gunderson family had tears streaming down their cheeks as they listened to Sarah relate the details of her vision. It was heartbreaking for them to hear their beautiful sister describe a preview of her own funeral, but there was a strange kind of luminosity about her face that eased the sadness of the narrative. It seemed as though Sarah knew that she was going to die and that her vision sought to achieve the purpose of attempting to accustom her family to the sad event as gently as possible.

As soon as Sarah had completed the account of her visionary experience, she confessed to some weakness, but she still wished to sit upright in bed and to visit with her older siblings, whom she had not seen for many months.

For the rest of the afternoon she was totally rational and appeared to suffer no debilitating pains. Other than an unnatural pallor and an admitted weakness, there seemed to be no indication that she was dying.

Toward evening the family was beginning to rejoice at what appeared to be a turn for the better in Sarah's sudden illness. Dr. Gunderson knew better, but he kept his sad awareness to himself.

In the early evening Sarah suffered a dramatic setback. She experienced violent muscle spasms, and her face grew taut with pain. Her skin blanched, and her larynx ceased to function.

Their transient hopes dashed, the Gunderson family reluctantly gave up all expectations of Sarah's recovery. They were forced to accept the fact that she was dying.

After what seemed to be an interminable period of time in which Sarah's body was tortured by terrible spasms, she at last lay still and closed her eyes. She emitted a deep sigh, then moved no more.

Dr. Gunderson solemnly checked his daughter's pulse and nodded in mute answer to the rest of the family's fears. Benumbed with grief, no one stirred.

Then it happened. The miracle. Or whatever it was.

The pretty young girl had just breathed her last, and her family had gathered mournfully around her pale, still body. Then all at once a deep, masculine voice issued forth from the girl and proceeded to give them instructions on how to revive the body.

"Take both of her arms and rub them as hard as you can!" ordered a rather gruff voice.

The body, just pronounced dead by a practicing physician, had opened its mouth. Its lips were moving, and it was clear to everyone that the voice was issuing forth from the deceased Sarah.

"Hurry!" the voice demanded. "It was not yet her time. She is not to stay here with us. Take both of her arms at once and begin to rub them as hard as you can!"

Startled into compliance, the Gunderson family members found themselves obeying the command of the invisible task master. As if in a collective trance, they began to massage Sarah's lifeless limbs.

And then a different voice, one decidedly more musical and pleasant, began to speak: "Good. That's good. But you should be holding her upright!"

Increasingly confused and baffled, Dr. Gunderson gently raised the body of his daughter. Mrs. Gunderson hastily moved a supportive arm around Sarah's back.

The gruff voice was back. "If I could have her

legs moved around so she could be set up on the footboard, I think she might be all right."

With a helpless shrug Dr. Gunderson attempted to effect the unusual request.

But he did not move quickly enough for the unseen advisers, and the entire family watched in awe as an invisible force lifted both of Sarah's legs and placed them on the footboard. One of the younger children began to whimper softly.

And now a *third* voice spoke up to contradict the previous order. "Really, now, don't you think the body should be allowed to rest on its back again? Please, let's move it back to the previous position."

Once again the unseen power present in the room acted without hesitation. Simultaneously, it nudged Dr. Gunderson out of the way and gently lowered Sarah's body to its original position on the bed. There it lay, once more silent and inert.

The bewildered Gunderson family stared at Sarah's body, by this time uncertain what would follow. No one dared moved for fear of other commands from the unseen trio of angels or spirits in the room.

Nothing happened for nearly fifteen minutes. Then a fourth voice began to speak softly to them.

"I know this has all seemed very strange to you," the gentle speaker admitted. "But a mistake had been made, and we were sent to correct it. You see, Sarah is not to stay here with us. It is not yet her time. Things got a little mixed up, and we had to correct matters. Sarah will be fine, and she will soon be awakened and placed back among you."

Incredibly, the unseen angel continued to counsel and to converse with the Gunderson family for nearly three hours. It described many aspects of the heavenly kingdom and advised them to maintain a prayer vigil around Sarah's body until she regained consciousness.

At last the invisible entity bade them farewell, and all was silent in the room.

Dr. Gunderson checked Sarah's pulse and found it beating feebly. Everyone could see that she was breathing in slow, measured breaths. With tears of joy soon replacing those of sorrow, they were comforted and elated to know that the unidentified visitors from the unseen world had really spoken truthfully when they said Sarah would return to them. The Gundersons decided that their strange guests must truly have been angelic messengers.

The family gathered around Sarah's bed and obeyed the soft-spoken angel's final command that they maintain a prayer vigil until she returned to consciousness.

It was nearly dawn before their sister awakened from the trancelike state that had held her for so many hours.

Although she underwent a rather long period of convalescence, Sarah truly had returned to her family from the dead. The astonishing physical ministrations and manipulations of the unseen spirits had managed to restore her heaven-bound soul to her Earth-held body.

· 12 ·

Children Who Painted Scenes of Their Heavenly Visits

Famed Bible scholar George M. Lamsa, who has spent years translating the gospels into English from their original Aramaic, has commented that human language cannot adequately convey spiritual ideas, visions, or images. There simply are no words that can measure, describe, or explain the essence of a spiritual occurrence such as a near-death or an illumination experience.

The Aramaic term *Khizwa* means to see something in the realm of spirit, as in a vision. *Giliana*, revelation, means to perceive that which is hidden from the eyes of the flesh but visible to the eyes of the spirit. In the dimension of spirit there exists neither time nor space, and spiritual concepts are eternal, universal, and free of all physical limitations. Therefore, spiritual experiences are incapable of being communicated by the human tongue, and they must often be explained only in parables, poetry, figurative speech, painting, or music.

Judi Bertoia, a former professor at the University of British Columbia, has collected beautiful pictures of Heaven painted by Rachel, a nine-year-old who died of leukemia, in the book *Drawings from a Dying Child*.

The paintings were inspired by Rachel's many out-of-body visits to Heaven before the cruel disease sent her to stay forever with God and the angels. The brave little girl said that she had been to heaven and she knew what it looked like. It was so beautiful and so colorful.

In spite of three grueling years of chemotherapy and radiation treatments, which brought on awful headaches and times of depression and panic, Rachel continued to capture on paper the vivid scenes that she observed in the other world.

According to Professor Bertoia, Rachel slipped into a comalike state on many occasions, and each time her doctors revived her, she proceeded to draw the colorful images that she had witnessed as she moved between life and death.

Rachel once explained that the colors in heaven were so bright and clear because there was no pollution there. She added that children were able to notice such things because they were closer to God and they hadn't been on Earth as long as grown-ups.

Before she died, Rachel expressed her wish that God would one day make her a child's guardian angel. She wanted to be able to be there to hug little kids and to hold their hands when they needed extra love.

A doctor we'll name Michael Worthen, a physician who practices pediatrics in the Omaha, Nebraska, area, told us of a case involving a ten-year-old boy that had a happier resolution than Rachel's.

"Jimmy Ludke had been involved in a hunting accident in which he had been wounded and his older brother, Samuel, had been killed," Dr. Worthen said. "Tragically, Sam had fallen on the .12-gauge shotgun that he had been cradling as he crawled over a fence. The blast had blown away a large portion of his face, and numerous pellets of shot had traveled behind him to strike Jimmy in his face and neck. He had lost a lot of blood and was in a comalike state before he was brought to an emergency room."

Jimmy remained mute and withdrawn. He would not even speak to his parents.

"It quickly became apparent that he had worshipped his seventeen-year-old brother. Samuel had taken Jimmy along hunting pheasants, and it was the first time that the two brothers had been allowed to go hunting alone without their father or uncle. Jimmy was absolutely devastated by the loss of his brother. He was unable to attend the funeral, and even though it was a closed-casket ceremony, it was just as well that he was not subject to the additional trauma."

Even after a week in the hospital, Jimmy was showing no improvement. His wounds had not been that bad. It was as if he had simply lost the will to live.

"One day as I was doing my rounds, I noticed that Jimmy had been doodling on the back of a get-well card that someone had sent him. When his parents came for visiting hours, I found out that Jimmy had always liked to sketch and draw. I instructed one of the nurses to leave a sketch pad and some colored pencils at his bedside table. Perhaps he would begin to 'talk' to us through his drawings."

The next afternoon Dr. Worthen was rather distressed to discover a drawing that he considered quite dark and morbid. Two young men or boys, covered with bloody wounds, were lying in a ditch while vultures circled overhead. Insects, worms, and snakes were crawling over the bodies of the two boys. Jimmy had entitled his drawing, "Sammy and Jimmy Go to Hell."

They had been feeding Jimmy intravenously, because he refused to eat. That night around midnight he began to run a very high fever and lapsed into a comalike state.

"One of the nurses on duty called me at home to report that it appeared as though little Jimmy Ludke had decided to pull the plug on himself. All of his vital signs were suddenly nose-diving. I told her to call his parents. Since visiting hours had been over for quite some time, I knew that they would be back home. I said that I would be there as soon as I could."

The crisis didn't pass for Jimmy Ludke until about four-thirty that morning.

"He suddenly opened his eyes and began to cry. He clutched his mother's hand and spoke for the first time since before the accident: 'Mom! Dad! I saw Sammy, and he's all right. He's in heaven with the angels, and he's okay. He didn't go to hell, after all.'"

The Ludkes wept openly and hugged their son and each other in warm embraces. "We didn't want to lose both our boys," they told Dr. Worthen and the attending nurse, as if having to explain their open and unrestrained emotion. "Thank God, Jimmy has come back to us."

Jimmy's assertion that he had seen Sammy in heaven was overlooked in the Ludkes' rejoicing and the medical personnel's triumph over death.

It wasn't until a couple of days later that Dr. Worthen really paid much attention to Jimmy's new pieces of artwork. In one drawing he had used bright colors to depict a taller boy shaking hands with a smaller one. A half dozen angels in white robes and bright golden halos stood around the two, smiling and singing in obvious approval.

"I really saw him, Dr. Worthen," Jimmy told him, his expansive smile a welcome replacement for the expressionless mask of the previous days. "I saw Sammy and talked to him, and he told me that he was all right. He didn't have to go to hell. Even the angels told me that Sammy could stay with them."

Dr. Worthen wanted to know why Jimmy had been so concerned about his older brother going to hell.

"Just because" was all that the doctor could get out of Jimmy before he went back to drawing another picture of a being that he said was Sammy's special guardian angel.

Dr. Worthen told us that it took an attractive young candy-striper, one of the volunteer high school girls, to get the full story out of Jimmy.

It seemed that just a couple of weeks before Sam's fatal accident, Mrs. Ludke had accompanied her husband on an out-of-town business trip, leaving the boys alone for the weekend on their own best behavior. Seventeen-year-old Sammy had yielded to temptation and invited two of his best buddies over to drink beer while they watched a late movie on television.

Although they thought that Jimmy was sound asleep before they popped the first bottle cap, the shocked ten-year-old came charging into the recreation room fulminating as though he were a temperance worker enforcing Prohibition.

"You're not old enough to drink beer," he scolded. "Mom and Dad would have a bird! Shame on you. Do you want to go to hell?"

Sammy and his friends found little Jimmy's outburst to be the most hilarious thing they had ever seen. Emboldened by the two bottles of beer that they had already imbibed, they told the ten-year-old that they didn't care if they went to hell or not. In fact, they had heard that beer was free in hell, courtesy of the devil.

Jimmy was stunned to the point of stuttering, a nervous habit that he thought he had conquered by the end of second grade.

"Hey, come on, Jim, my man." Sam sought to pacify him. "Aren't we the tightest two brothers in the world?"

Jimmy agreed that was true, but Sammy still shouldn't be drinking beer and talking about going to hell.

"But if you are my tight and true little brother, man, then you would follow me even to hell. Am I not right?"

Sammy's friends agreed. Jimmy should be so loyal to his big brother that he would follow him to hell if need be.

At last Jimmy nodded and took Sammy's hand in their secret grip.

"Swear on it, little brother. Swear that you would follow me to hell. And swear that you will absolutely, positutely *never* tell Mom and Dad that we were drinking beer here tonight."

Jimmy swore to it, but he lay awake most of the night worrying about the dangers of such a pact. What was beer bravado to a trio of seventeen-year-olds was a solemn oath to an impressionable ten-year-old.

Jimmy had continued to dog his brother about the dangers of tempting the devil, joking about hell, and drinking beer while still a minor.

In fact, on the day of the accident when Sammy had invited his little brother along on their first solo hunt, Jimmy had wanted to know if Sam was going to bring along some beer.

"Of course not!" Sam had growled at him. "It's stupid to mix alcohol and gunpowder. And don't start up with that crap about my going to hell. Later on, if I want to have a beer with the guys, I'll do it. And if I do go to hell, little brother, then I am going to take you with me!"

Dr. Worthen shook his head in silent contemplation before he concluded his account.

"That offhand remark of Sam's had been what had nearly caused his loyal little brother to starve himself or to will himself to death so that he could follow the brother that he idolized so much to the very gates of Hades. It really makes you think about making careless jokes or uttering flippant statements that you don't really mean, doesn't it?"

Dr. Worthen pointed at a framed drawing of a large angel with his arms around two boys. "Jimmy still draws pictures of angels. Thank God, he believed that he saw Sam in heaven, happy and harmonious. And who's to say he didn't? Sure beats all that talk about hell, anyway."

• 13 •

Near-Death Experiences of the Very Young

Dr. Melvin Morse, author of such books as *Closer to the Light* and *Transformed by the Light*, has remarked that the near-death experiences of children are special because children talk from the heart and are relatively free of cultural contamination. When children relate an account of an NDE, they do so simply, purely, unfiltered. And they are more unlikely to have an undeclared agenda of proving a particular religious belief or a preconceived spiritual expectation.

Many children describe going into the Light and then being told by a heavenly entity to go back because it is not yet their time to stay on the other side. Other children have said that they were given a choice and were able to make their own decision whether or not to stay in another level of reality.

Dr. Morse has observed that it is the wise child who returns understanding that life has a purpose. As one near-death patient told him, "Life is for living. The Light is for later."

Even after so many years of researching the endlessly fascinating phenomenon of near-death experiences, we continue to be intrigued by the extreme youth of some of the children reporting NDEs.

In his book *In Search of the Dead,* Jeffrey Iverson, the host of a British television series on the paranormal, tells of a five-year-old boy who startled his parents by recounting a near-death experience he had survived at the age of nine months. Indeed, the youngster's heart had stopped in the hospital while he was an infant. His parents certainly knew that, but they were completely unaware of their son's extraordinary experience at that time.

He told them that he remembered crawling down a tunnel toward a bright light. He saw doctors and nurses, his grandfather and his mother below him, but a kind of wall separated them from him.

After he crawled through the tunnel for quite some time, a helping hand lifted him up to a place where the light was extremely bright. He was no longer crawling, but gliding or floating.

He remembered seeing crowds of white figures, golden roads, and even God. The boy said that God had spoken to him telepathically and asked him if he wanted to return.

Although he told God that he wanted to stay in the Light, God informed him that he had a purpose in life and needed to return. And then the infant was back in the hospital—where he was in a coma for three months.

The boy's parents told Iverson that their son's startling disclosure came about quite innocently one day during lunchtime conversation when Mark asked them, "Did you know I died?"

Their immediate response was, "Oh, really?" but Mark went on to supply such an extraordinary amount of details concerning his surgery, the environment of the hospital room, and descriptions of medical personnel that they became convinced that their son had truly been observing the events which occurred when he was nine months old from an out-of-body vantage point.

Dr. David Smith, associate professor of pediatrics at the University of British Columbia, told journalist Esmond Choueke of the case of four-year-old Sandra and three-year-old Chrissy, two young cancer victims who were reunited in the spirit world.

According to Dr. Smith, the two girls had met while they were being treated for leukemia in a hospital cancer ward. Sandra was sent home to spend her final days with her family, and she was unaware that Chrissy had died.

Two days after Chrissy's death, Sandra fell into a deep coma, and when she regained consciousness, she told her mother that she had seen Chrissy in heaven. Sandra had at first been frightened in the celestial surroundings, but her friend had told her not to be afraid; she was there to guide her.

Dr. Smith said that it was impossible for Sandra to know of Chrissy's death. The two little friends were miles apart and had been separated for months without any contact.

After her near-death visit to heaven, Sandra became "calm and peaceful," stated Dr. Smith, who treated both girls at Vancouver General Hospital. Sandra told him that she had gone to a place of beautiful white light, and she knew that everything would be all right, because Crissy was there waiting for her.

Sandra gradually lost consciousness and died the following day.

"She had no fear of dying," Dr. Smith commented. "Chrissy's death took on special meaning—she was to guide another troubled child who was to die soon after."

Forty-two-year-old John Lione of Brooklyn, New York, has recently recalled a near-death experience that occurred to him during his birth.

"My mother said my birth was a difficult one. I

was what they call a 'blue baby.' They didn't bring me to her for two days. My face was all black and blue, and I had two black eyes. She said it looked like the skin had been pulled off my face. That was where the forceps had cut me up. They had to give me a tracheotomy so I could breathe. I am also completely deaf in my right ear. As if all that was not enough, I came down with measles when I was about six months old."

From his earliest childhood John could remember a recurring dream that always began and ended in the same way.

"I would be kneeling down, all bent over. I am frantically trying to untie knots in some kind of rope. I am just starting to get free of the rope when I get punched in the face."

At first little John would wake up crying. Later, as he became conditioned to the nightmare, he would be able to sleep through the part with the knots, the rope, and the punch.

"The dream would then go on to the part where I can see this bright light coming at me from my right. Then, when I look to my left, I see this woman in a long, flowing gown. I cannot see her features clearly, but I know that she is not my mother. At the same time, I know that I know her. I also feel a great urgency to reach her. I call and call to her, but I can't seem to get to her. And that's where the dream would end."

For years John told the repetitive dream to friends and to health care professionals. No one seemed to have a clue as to what particular meaning the dream held for him.

In 1986 he had his gall bladder removed, and he experienced the bizarre dream for the last time.

John had decided that the nightmare of ropes and knots and floating women in gowns and bright lights would always remain one of his personal mysteries when he chanced across a copy of Dr. Melvin Morse's book *Closer to the Light* in a most peculiar way.

"I was walking to work on a rainy day when I saw this book lying on the ground, dry, like someone had just dropped it. I didn't see anyone around who might be its owner, so I picked it up.

"That night when I started reading it, I was amazed to find stories of children who had had weird dreams somewhat similar to mine. My wife said that maybe I hadn't been dreaming after all. Maybe I had been having a memory of a near-death experience. The rope with the knots was when I struggled in the womb with the umbilical cord. Getting punched in the face is when the doctor grabbed me with the forceps. Then I believe that I died—and after that I went into the light."

Sometime later, John attended a conference at which Betty Eadie, author of *Embraced by the Light,* was speaking and relating her own near-death experiences.

"Afterward, when I was speaking to Betty, she mentioned seeing heavenly beings spinning material out of some bright substance. Dr. P.M.H. Atwater was there, and she said that she believed the substance to be 'spun light.' That's when I knew what the woman in the long, flowing gown had been wearing. It was a gown made of 'spun light.' "

Dr. P.M.H. Atwater told us of a case that she had investigated in which a four-year-old boy reported a near-death experience after having drowned and been resuscitated.

"His mother may have been somewhat skeptical until he told her that he had met his brother while he was on the other side. 'Brother, honey?' she questioned him. 'You know that you don't have a brother.'

"Her little boy totally shocked her when he replied, 'Yes, I do, Mommy. He was pulled from your tummy when you were only fourteen.'

"The woman was stunned. It was true. She had become pregnant and had an abortion when she was fourteen. She had never told anyone—not her husband, not even her parents."

· 14 ·

Touching the Sacred Space of God

In her role as an ordained Protestant minister and as a family and crisis counselor, Sherry Hansen Steiger has always believed that she was able to be an extremely effective guide to those children who suffered traumatic aftereffects of an NDE, because she was able to relate so well to their confusion and distress. Sherry, you see, has herself undergone six near-death experiences, three before she was ten.

Sherry supposes that she first left the Earth plane on a temporary visit to other dimensions when she was months old and nearly died of pneumonia.

Her second excursion to the other side occurred

at the age of six, when she was in a coma during a severe bout of rheumatic fever.

At the age of nine, medical personnel accidentally gave her an overdose of ether when she was in the hospital to have her tonsils removed.

When she was twenty-four, Sherry survived a shark attack off the coast of South Padre Island, Texas.

She was twenty-eight when she suffered a heart "episode" and was told by three eminent cardiologists that she must have surgery at once—or die within twenty-four hours.

At the age of thirty, a kidney infection sent her temperature soaring to 106 degrees—and her spirit spiraling to other universes.

"There is absolutely no question in my mind that my childhood near-death experiences had a profound affect on the choice of my life path as a minister, a social reformer, and a spiritual seeker and teacher," Sherry said. "As strange as it may seem to some, I can recall looking out from behind the bars of my crib after my near-death with pneumonia and feeling that I, as Brad stated after his NDE, was a stranger here on Earth. I can remember thinking that people on Earth weren't supposed to be behaving the way I saw them acting."

After slipping in and out of her body many times during her long siege with rheumatic fever, Sherry mostly recalls the shapes, lights, and geometric patterns she observed in some other dimension of reality.

"I had dreams of those brightly colored geometric shapes for years," she said. "Dreams that would often turn into nightmarish experiences. The shapes would rush at me at tremendous rates of speed, but sometimes it would seem as though I were soaring toward the shapes down some kind of long tunnel. The sense of movement would grow faster and faster, and then it would seem to me as if the shapes were somehow pushing against me, exerting great pressure on my body. It was at that point that I would often scream for my mother, who was never able to make any sense of my bad dream of 'lights and colors pressing on me.'"

When she was eight years old and attending a summer camp in upper Michigan, she was privileged to see a dramatic manifestation of the angel that she had felt around her ever since her NDE during rheumatic fever. Several other girls, who probably were not quite prepared for such an otherworldly visitation, also witnessed the appearance of the heavenly figure.

The angelic being appeared to come down through the ceiling of the cabin in which Sherry was staying, and most of the startled girls went down on their knees and folded their hands in prayer.

"She emanated a brilliant bluish-white light,"

Sherry recalled. "She appeared to be the most loving, beautiful, and gentle woman imaginable."

Sherry and a few of the other girls heard the angelic being tell them how very special they each were and how very much God loved them. There were other messages, but memory has dimmed most of them.

Sherry's eyes were brimming with tears, and she saw that many of her friends were also weeping.

After the angel had vanished, Sherry sensed that on some level of her consciousness she had been given important insights into the sacredness, interconnectedness, and oneness of all of God's creation.

When she was accidentally given an overdose of ether during a tonsilectomy at the age of nine, Sherry had the sensation of moving toward a wondrous light.

"When I recovered from that NDE, I had a distinct knowledge that there were other dimensions of being that were to be taken seriously.

"I really felt like a stranger in a strange land after this experience. I would go off by myself and sit in the woods near our home in Minnesota and become completely enraptured by the patterns that I would see everywhere present in nature.

"I still had the bizarre dreams of the brightly colored geometric shapes zooming toward me, and I now began to notice fascinating geometric designs all around me. I began to observe the incredible harmony that seemed inherent in these natural designs and patterns."

Often during her ministerial counseling sessions with troubled children, Sherry would make the remarkable discovery that they also had experienced terrible dreams of lights and colored shapes rushing at them. Gently probing further, she would invariably find that these children had also experienced NDEs when they were younger. Very often their memories of the other side had been repressed and had expressed themselves in these terrible nightmares of hurtling through space.

"My being able to share my own near-death experiences and my recognition of the geometric shapes and lights took a lot of the 'scary' feelings out of these young people's trauma. In many cases I was able to replace a sense of the frightening with a sense of the holy.

"The fact that I could relate to these kids on such a highly personal level and share with them a secret that they had largely kept hidden from everyone else for fear of ridicule gave us a unique kind of commonality. I was the minister, the counselor, yet I, too, had experienced leaving the body and visiting other dimensions of reality. The sharing of such intimate spiritual confidences allowed me to forge a bond with them that allowed them to come to peace in a way that I doubt would otherwise have been possible. As unorthodox as it may seem to other clergy persons or psychological counselors, I was able to utilize the near-death experience as a therapeutic device."

It was not until 1968 or '69, when Sherry saw the motion picture *2001: A Space Odyssey*, that she perceived anything like the geometric patterns and lights that she had seen moving rapidly toward her. There, in the amazing "light show" sequence when the astronaut Bowman is poised to approach Jupiter, she saw an amazingly accurate cinematic representation/re-creation of the personalized "light show" that she had seen since she was a small child.

"The viewing of this movie triggered other memories of my childhood near-death experiences. I remembered walking through many other dimensional doorways. That one incredible sequence in Stanley Kubrick's masterpiece of cinema was like a healing, magical balm to my spirit. Those memories that had haunted and confused me for so long now seemed a great deal less frightening."

During the shark attack that she experienced just a short time before seeing *2001*, Sherry was pulled under the surface of the water three times by her monstrous adversary.

"I had seen the horror in the faces of swimmers coming to rescue me before the huge 'something' grabbed me for the second time. I thought I would surely die. I saw those same sparks of light and colorful shapes zooming toward me.

"I found out later when the sea park ranger pulled a shark's tooth from my foot that the monster must have been toying with me before it made me its main dinner course. When it pulled me under for the third time, I was shown a review of all the major scenes of my life. It is just incredible to think how you can see all of your life in what is perhaps only two or three seconds of linear time.

"Surely I would have drowned if I had even suspected my sea attacker was a shark! At the time, all I thought was a very *big* fish!"

It was later theorized that it could have been a team of dolphins that arrived on the scene to save Sherry from being an entree for a monster of the deep. *Something* made the shark release her, and someone managed to pull her onto shore. She awakened in a first aid station, her legs scraped raw by the shark's rough skin and covered with blood.

After the ranger pulled out the shark's tooth embedded in her left foot, he immediately issued a shark warning and cleared the beaches of all swimming.

When she "froze" while she was serving at a dinner party at age twenty-eight, she was rushed to a hospital where three cardiologists advised her that she must submit to immediate open-heart surgery or die within twenty-four hours.

"Because I was more out of my body than in it, I was able to see a much wider spectrum of reality. I could somehow understand that their diagnosis, though well intentioned, was *not* the true story. In this state of extended awareness, I did accept their evaluation that I had a hole in my heart that had been precipitated by my childhood bout with rheumatic fever, but I *knew* that such dramatic surgery as they were prescribing was totally unnecessary. I thanked them for their concern—and checked myself out of the hospital."

When she later submitted to additional testing, Sherry learned that her intuitive assessment had been correct. It would have been unnecessary to have her chest opened. While the hole in her heart was truly present, it was, in reality, miniscule compared to how it must have sounded to the doctors' stethoscopes. Somehow, the sound had been amplified, thereby causing the leak in her heart to seem larger than it really was.

When Sherry was stricken with a kidney infection that sent her temperature to 106 degrees, the near-fatal boiling point for an adult, she was unable to check herself out of the hospital, for she was in and out of a comatose state for ten days. When she flickered back into consciousness, she found that she had been packed in ice with "all kinds of tubes hooked up" to her.

"I truly gained an appreciation for the kinds of altered states of consciousness during this time. Perhaps this time in a coma was, on some other level of reality, a time of deep teaching for me. All of my near-death experiences as a child seemed to be somehow synthesized in this encounter with the other side.

"Although I was in a terribly weakened physical condition when I left the hospital, I knew that my time on other planes of consciousness had shown me that all of the many disparate things that had occurred to me during my life on Earth did have meaning and a purpose. And I felt drawn to spend more time researching various spiritual paths and the scientific disciplines that might cast greater understanding on the techniques and applications of these ancient wisdoms."

Sherry began to practice meditation seriously, and it was during an astonishing five-hour meditative experience in 1985 that she was given the spiritual impetus to pull together all the scattered memories of her childhood near-death experiences and to gain special meaning for the remainder of her Earth walk.

She remembered that her Real Self was met by an angelic Light Being who escorted her through a beautiful mystical adventure. Although she issued an immediate disclaimer that no words can ever come close to describing what she saw, she states that, audacious as it may sound to many, she truly felt as though she saw or touched the sacred space of God.

Sherry said that the Light Being who guided her through the experience was loving and caring.

"The Being did not seem to have a gender, but I felt as though I knew him/her."

She was in a place that perhaps could best be described as a diamond or crystal city (or planet) where she beheld unearthly beauty and colors and lights much different from those on Earth. Later, she recalled that during numerous counseling sessions, she had heard many children attempting to describe to her something similar that they had seen in their near-death experiences.

"Maybe I beheld the New Jerusalem. Its beauty was beyond anything I've ever dreamed possible. It was like a crystal or diamond planet, reflecting and refracting the purest, most brilliant colors. The light all around was effervescent, as if it were alive. As if the light itself was alive and that light was the very essence of *love*. This love was deeper and more complete than anything experienced here on Earth. I myself seemed to become a living crystal, and I became fused with the light. I became the Light."

This dramatic visionary experience became a life mission for her. Sherry became more compelled than ever before to tell everyone that God's promise to humankind is, indeed, *real*. Life does continue after death.

"The most important thing in life that we can do is to be loving and to meet all experiences with love," she said.

Shortly after she received the powerful vision, she was led to research what was eventually to become known as fractal geometry, a "new" mathematics. By 1988 she had assembled a powerful multimedia presentation utilizing slides and computer-derived images of fractals that evolved into remarkably effective healing seminars.

In his *One with the Light,* Brad states how it was not until he had viewed Sherry's presentation that he saw designs which closely approximated the geometric images that he had been shown during his own childhood near-death experience.

In addition to testifying that the viewing of such images prompted tears to their eyes and healing energy in their physical bodies, numerous seminar participants said that the geometric shapes had also triggered memories of their own earlier near-death experiences, which they had not been able to put into words until they had experienced Sherry's presentation. Many of these individuals stated that they, too, had experienced dreams or nightmares as children in which they had seen "shapes of light" coming at them.

"Somehow, my out-of-body viewing of the New Jerusalem—or whatever it truly was—filled me with a wonderful sense of oneness with All-That-Is and allowed me to visit the dimension of spirit from which my soul had come to Earth," Sherry said. "Perhaps that is the true spiritual home for all of us—a place we call 'Heaven' where we truly shall be one with God . . . one with love."

• 15 •

Extrasensory Aftereffects

Numerous researchers have discovered that both adults and children who are survivors of a near-death experience may develop extraordinary paranormal abilities. Parapsychologists as well as medical personnel interested in the subject of NDE have recorded such phenomena as people who emitted a force so strong that it could stop watches; people who acquired a superintelligence and were suddenly psychic; people who were gifted with the incredible ability to heal themselves and others.

Dr. P.M.H. Atwater told us that in her extensive research into the near-death experience she would estimate that seventy percent of those people who declare themselves to be psychics, clairvoyants, channelers, or otherwise gifted with extrasensory abilities had an NDE as a child.

Earlier in this book, we indicated that the results of our questionnaire of paranormal and mystical experiences revealed that sixty-four percent of our respondents—many of whom claim paranormal talents—said that they had undergone an NDE, eighty-two percent of them before the age of twelve.

Brad recalled that back in 1967, when he was collecting data and conducting interviews for the survey that would evolve into the present questionnaire, he encountered only one professional psychic-sensitive who claimed *not* to have undergone a near-death or visionary out-of-body experience. All of the others freely acknowledged an NDE at some time in their lives—and the great majority claimed such astral adventures in their childhood.

One such mind traveler claimed that for nine months, as his teenage body lay ill with sleeping sickness, he accomplished many journeys in his astral body and saw many things that he could later verify.

Herewith are a number of comments from those respondents to our questionnaire who underwent NDEs as children and who immediately noticed pronounced changes in their lives:

NDE survivor affects anything electrical

"I affect all electrical appliances. My presence causes malfunctions with telephones, dishwashers, blenders, juicers, movie projectors, and lamps. All my cars soon develop electrical problems when I begin to drive them."

Unable to wear watches, even gliches microchips

"I have messed up everything electronic in nature at one point or another. I have never been able to wear watches except for quartz-crystal types. I've even ruined digitals. Every car that I have ever owned has experienced severe electrical problems. Microchip memories lose their data around me. I have even found that walking or driving under some street lamps can cause them to switch off for no apparent reason. The electronic phone in my office at work often goes haywire, thus causing disturbances through the entire system."

Doctors puzzled by effect on electromagnetic equipment

"Physicians have often been frankly puzzled as to how to treat my physical needs. Some have been intrigued with the effect that I have on electromagnetic equipment, as well as the effect that it has on me."

Able to "hear" electricity, excels at guessing games

"After my near-death experience at the age of ten, I have been able to 'hear' electricity. Television sets go crazy if I walk or stand near them. I have had numerous out-of-body experiences, and I excel at any kind of ESP 'guessing games.'"

Hypersensitivity to light, colors, sound

"Not only did my near-death experience leave me with a high degree of paranormal ability, but my physical senses also seemed to be extended. I have an acute hypersensitivity to sound, light, touch, colors, and emotions. My hearing is so sensitive that any loud noise over thirty seconds in duration can set up an inner vibration that causes me great pain in the mastoid area, then causes uncontrolled shaking which can last for several minutes."

Accurate clairvoyant visions and precognitive dreams

"I have had accurate clairvoyant visions ever since recovering from the illness that brought me my near-death experience when I was nine. I often have dreams that accurately predict future events."

Receives automatic writing from higher dimensions

"Ever since I 'died' at the age of eleven and was made to understand that there really is no death, only a change of worlds, I have kept in touch with the guiding spirits that I met on the other side through the process of automatic writing. At first I received messages that I wrote out in longhand on legal-sized notebook tablets. Since I learned to type, I simply sit down in front of my word processor and say, 'All right, guys,' and thought transference from the higher dimensions will channel through me."

High degree of telepathic and precognitive abilities

"I survived a near-fatal automobile accident when I was fourteen, and even before I left the hospital, I noticed that I had a high degree of telepathic ability. I also began to have prophetic dreams. I accurately predicted my grandfather's death in a freeway accident, and for years after that my conventionally religious family believed my ESP abilities to be of Satan."

Astounding degree of telepathic control

"I nearly died of rheumatic fever when I was six, and up to the age of sixteen I could practice and control telepathy to an astounding degree. I still have a lot of ESP experiences, and so do my children. Each of my children, by the way, have been tested to have extremely high intelligence."

Headaches precede major catastrophes

"I had a feeling there would be a bad earthquake somewhere in California when the San Francisco quake occurred because I had had a severe headache all day. When some catastrophe is about to happen, I can usually 'feel' it before it happens. I have a terrible headache, and it won't go away. When the disaster happens . . . then it goes away."

The study of near-death experiences throughout the decades has produced a unique vocabulary during the many various efforts to describe literally or figuratively the non-physical process that occurs to the human body, mind, and spirit.

Dr. Robert Crookall, the British geologist and botanist, a pioneer in the study of near-death and out-of-body experiences, refers to that aspect of ourselves that somehow is able to separate from the physical body and return to it as the astral body, the etheric body, and sometimes as the Soul Body.

Dr. Crookall theorized that the Soul Body does consist of matter, "but it is extremely subtle and may be described as 'super-physical.'"

Much was made in earlier studies of the "silver cord" that many out-of-body experiencers describe as somehow connecting their Soul Body to their physical body. The American student of astral traveling, Sylvan Muldoon, reported that he had often seen "a kind of elastic string" connecting his two bodies. The term and/or concept itself was inspired by the poetic passages in *Ecclesiastes* [12:5–7], which many scholars have taken to refer to the reality of our spiritual bodies and our innate ability to separate spirit from flesh:

> . . . *Because man goeth to his long home, and the mourners go about the streets. Or ever the silver cord be loosed or the golden bowl be broken, or the pitcher be broken at the fountain, or the wheel be broken at the cistern. Then shall the dust return to the earth as it was: and the spirit shall return unto God who gave it.*

Dr. Crookall speculated that the silver cord may correspond to the umbilical cord in childbirth— where an old body gives birth to a new body. To sever the cord, he theorized, would undoubtedly mean death. In near-death, Dr. Crookall suggested that the silver cord would be "attenuated to such an extent that it transmits almost no vitality."

Quoting a number of people who have had near-death experiences, Dr. Crookall reported being told that one man felt the pull of his cord "as though it were made of stout elastic." A woman observed that as her Soul Body neared the physical shell, the cord became "shorter and thicker," as would be expected from such an extension.

Nadine Pleason of Mesa, Arizona, may have expressed the concept of the silver cord aptly, as well as poetically, in the December 1994 issue of *The Omega New Age Directory*:

> The Silver Cord
> connects me to the lifeline
>   of all existence.
> The Silver Cord
> allows me to experience
>   beyond my senses.
> The parting of the Silver Cord
> allows my soul to drift upward
>   to the heavenly realms.
> The Silver Cord of Life.
> The Eternal Silver Cord.

Dr. Alexander Cannon, the "Master-the-Fifth of the Great White Lodge of the Himalayas, Kushog Vogi of Northern Tibet," saw the various strata of our physical and non-physical selves a bit differently. In Dr. Cannon's cosmology, the astral body

surrounds the physical body "like an egg-shell surrounds the egg within it and is linked up with the
physical body by invisible vibrations on the ether
in the air being carried to the mind centers on the
plexuses of the involuntary nervous system." In his
view, the astral body is the scriptural "golden bowl"
and the etheric body is the linking "silver cord."

Dr. Cannon compares the etheric body to a
"streak of light running down the front of the spinal cord of the physical body, but independent of
either the astral or the physical body, whereas the
physical body is dependent, through the involuntary sympathetic nervous system, on the astral
body, and in turn, the astral body is dependent on
the etheric body."

According to Dr. Cannon, the East has long believed that when the physical body dies, the astral
body containing the etheric body separates from
the physical body after three days and that after
years, perhaps centuries, the astral body dies and
leaves only the etheric body to become a "spirit."

Such esoteric knowledge, he reminds his readers,
has been acquired by centuries of effort and experimentation by Eastern adepts. We of the West are
only beginning to become aware of the existence of
our psychic selves.

One well-known contemporary metaphysical
teacher who underwent a near-death journey as a
child and who lived to translate that experience
into a method of Soul Travel that evolved into a

controversial worldwide spiritual organization was the late Paul Twitchell.

As Twitchell told the story, he was only five years old, a small boy dying of pleurisy, when his stepsister healed him via astral projection. She slipped into his room late on the night that very likely would have been his last. She sat beside the bed in a lotus position, took a couple of deep breaths, and slipped out of her physical body into the *Atma Sarup,* the Soul Body.

"She took me out with her," Paul told Brad during one of their many interview sessions. "Both of us were in our Soul Bodies, and we hung off the ceiling like a pair of eyes viewing the body of the sick little boy on the bed below. My stepsister accomplished the healing of my physical body by impressing the thought that I would be made whole again upon both my astral and my physical body."

Once the spiritual essence of Paul knew that all was well and that the living clay below them on the bed would once again be his temple, he expressed a reluctance to reenter the body. He resisted for a moment, then his stepsister impressed upon him the necessity of returning.

In what seemed to be the very next moment, Paul remembered awakening to find his stepmother and the rest of the family standing by the bed, completely amazed at the swift recovery of their younger child.

Such a childhood experience launched Twitchell on a great spiritual pilgrimage that exposed him to the teachings of various Tibetan masters. By the late 1960s he had come to accept such matters as near-death experiences to be not at all bizarre or unusual. In fact, he believed that one could consciously learn to Soul Travel through meditative techniques rather than near-death traumas.

"Soul Travel is the natural means of going to God, and as such, it creates a joyous state in which one lives for all concerned—family, humankind, God," Twitchell said.

"It must be remembered, however," he continued, "that Soul Travel is concerned mainly with the movement of soul in the lower worlds, that of the regions from the physical planes to the fifth plane, which is the first of those ethereal regions named as the world of pure spirit. From there we are within the true kingdom and no longer need movement or travel. Soul is beyond time and space, which is existent within the lower planes, such as the physical, astral, causal, mental, and etheric planes.

"We find that as long as we are within the lower worlds, which are in time and space concepts, we are concerned with travel or movement, but when we reach the upper planes of God, there is no time or space. Travel is not needed, and we are in the state of total awareness, that is, God-realization, or absolute consciousness."

• 16 •

Some Classic Cases of Near-Death Research

As students of human experience and as spiritual seekers, we feel that it is always a good thing to remind ourselves that there truly is nothing new under the sun. And perhaps that old maxim applies to psychical research more than many other areas of human interest and exploration.

If serious students of spiritual matters will but take the time to examine the available literature of earlier researchers in the field, they will soon discover that many of the contemporary theories that are being touted as suggesting new truths or as presenting daringly innovative concepts are really very old ideas that have had their time of popularity and rejection more than once before. Some of the most ancient of metaphysical ideas and belief constructs seem to be discovered afresh by each succeeding generation, and many areas of spiritual enlightenment and insight gain, lose, and regain faddish popularity on the mass level of consciousness in what appear to be cyclical patterns of approval and dismissal.

While we may with some justification consider ourselves to be pioneers in various facets of phenomenology—including the investigation of near-death experiences—at least for our own generation, even a cursory examination of the literature of psychical research soon reminds us that we are traveling in the footsteps of those who have gone before. And—unless one pursues an area of research solely for personal ego satisfaction—such a discovery should prove to be gratifying, as well as humbling, for it automatically connects one with a timeless and universal brotherhood and sisterhood of fellow pilgrims on Earth who have undergone similar mystical and spiritual experiences.

The *Journal of the American Society for Psychical Research* for 1918 contains the remarkable account of a ten-year-old girl named Daisy Dryden, who during the last three days of her life in October 1864 experienced numerous out-of-body visits to the other side. Daisy, the daughter of David Anderson Dryden, a Methodist minister, encountered the spirit of her little brother Allie, who had died seven months before, and conversed with him as well as with many other spirit beings. The detailed record of the visions and heavenly scenes witnessed by the child were related by her mother shortly after Daisy's death.

Although the doctors had assured the Dryden family that Daisy would soon recover from her bout with typhoid fever, she told them that Allie had informed her that she would soon be joining him in the spirit world.

Then, expressing a kind of clairvoyance in which she appeared to be aware of both the physical and the nonphysical worlds, Daisy wondered aloud if she would still be able to visit her loved ones behind on the Earth plane.

"I'll ask Allie if it will be possible," she said to those friends and family members gathered around her bed.

After a brief pause she relayed her brother's answer: "He says that it is quite possible and that I shall return sometimes, but you will be unaware of my presence. Nevertheless, I shall be able to talk to you."

Two days before she died, Daisy's Sunday school teacher came to see her, and before she left, the well-intentioned lady said to the child: "My dear little Daisy, you are about to pass over the dark river."

When she had gone, Daisy asked her father what her teacher had meant by the dark river.

Reverend Dryden did his best to explain the

metaphor of a river to represent the dividing curtain between life and death.

"What nonsense!" his daughter exclaimed with a burst of derisive laughter. "There is no river here at all. There is no dividing curtain. There is not even a line between this world and the next."

Stretching out her little hand as if to indicate a clear pathway, she continued her description of the world beyond. "What is here is there. I know it is so, because I can see you all here, and I can see the others over there at the same time."

When Daisy's mother asked her to explain what she meant by her reference to "over there," the child said, "It is impossible for me to explain—it is so different from our world that I can't make you understand what I mean."

Her mother moved to her bedside and held her hand.

"Dear Mama, I wish you could see Allie." Daisy smiled. "He is quite close to you."

Instinctively, Mrs. Dryden turned around but Daisy continued: "He told me that you would not be able to see him, because your spiritual eyes are shut. I can see him, because my spirit is now tied to my body by a very fine thread of life."

The next day when her Sunday school teacher returned, Daisy informed the woman that her two children were present. The teacher's children had gone to the other side many years before, and if they had lived, they would have been nearly grown up. All of the adults present that day were quite certain that Daisy had never heard anyone speak of them, so she would not have known anything whatever about them before seeing them in the spirit world.

When her teacher asked Daisy to describe the children, she could not relate to the girl's descriptions of them. "You are describing grown-ups," she protested. "They were little children when they passed on."

Allie explained through Daisy that children did not stay children when they crossed to the other side. "They grow up, just as they do in this life."

The Sunday school teacher shook her head in wonder. "But my little daughter Mary fell and was so injured that she could not stand up straight."

Daisy smiled and assured her that her daughter was all right now: "She is straight and beautiful; and your son is looking so noble and happy."

In her report of Daisy's final days, Mrs. Dryden wrote that another family friend who came to pay her respects was informed that her daughter, who had died some years before, was also now an adult on the other side.

The mother could not recognize her from the description given until Daisy said, "She used to have a mole on the left side of her neck, but she does not have it now."

With this added bit of information, Mrs. Dryden declared, the woman was convinced.

Mrs. Dryden asked her daughter how she was

able to converse with Allie. "I don't hear you speak, nor do you move your lips."

Daisy smiled and replied: "We speak with our thoughts."

Mrs. Dryden wished to know in what form Allie appeared to her.

"He is not dressed as we are," Daisy explained. "His body is clothed in something dazzlingly white. It is wonderfully bright. Oh, Mama, you should see how fine, light, and splendid his robe is—and how very white!"

Reverend Dryden cited the psalmist who declared, "He is clothed with light."

"Oh, yes, father," she agreed. "That is very true."

Daisy loved to hear her sister Loulou sing some of her favorite hymns. In one particular stanza, when Loulou was singing about the wings of angels, Daisy began to giggle.

"Oh, Loulou, it is so funny. We were always told that angels had wings. But it is not so. It is a mistake. Angels do not have any wings at all."

Loulou found such an assertion difficult to accept. "But they must have wings, dear Daisy. Or else how could they fly down from Heaven?"

Daisy explained further: "They don't fly. They just come. Do you know, the very moment that I think of our brother Allie, he is here at once."

Mrs. Dryden, who had been listening to the conversation between her daughters, wanted to know how it was that Daisy managed to see the angels.

Daisy was quick to admit that she did not always see them. "But when I do, the walls seem to vanish and I can see ever so far away—and I see crowds and crowds of spirits. Those spirits who come close to me are those whom I knew in my life, but others I have never seen before."

On the day of her death, Daisy asked her mother for a hand mirror. Mrs. Dryden hesitated, fearing that the child might be horrified by her pinched and haggard features.

But after calmly considering her reflection in the looking glass for several minutes, Daisy said, "My poor body is used up, like one of Mama's old dresses that she hangs up in the wardrobe and never wears again.

"But I possess a spiritual body, which shall replace my old one. I have already got it on me, and it is with my spiritual eyes that I see the spirit world—even though my earthly body is still attached to the spiritual one. You will place my body in the grave, because I shall have no further use for it, but I shall be clothed in another body much more beautiful than this one—one just like Allie's!

"Mama, darling, don't cry, for if I have to go away, it is for my benefit. God knows what is best."

The child asked that she open the window for her, and Mrs. Dryden complied with her request.

"I want to have a last look at the beautiful world, for after the sunrise tomorrow I shall be no more."

Daisy requested that her father raise her up a little. "Good-bye, good-bye, my pretty world. I still love you, but, nevertheless, I don't wish to remain here any longer."

Mrs. Dryden's journal recorded that it was a quarter to eleven that night when Daisy called out to her father: "Papa, lift me up. Allie has come to look for me."

When the child had been placed as she wished, she asked that someone sing a hymn.

"Go and get Loulou," one of the adults in attendance at Daisy's bedside said. "She's the singer in the family."

"No," Daisy said in a soft voice. "Please don't disturb her. She's asleep."

Then, just as the hands of the clock pointed at eleven, Daisy lifted up her hands and said, "I'm coming, Allie!"

It was at that moment, Mrs. Dryden stated, that her daughter ceased to breathe.

The heavenly visions of Daisy Dryden made quite an impression upon psychical researchers of the day. Professor James H. Hyslop of Columbia University, author of *Science of a Future Life,* conducted a full investigation of the case and reported that he could confirm every detail. Professor Bozzano quoted the case in his *Phenomenes Psychiques,* [*circa* 1923] as did George Lindsay Johnson in his *Does Man Survive?* [1936].

In his summation of the Daisy Dryden case, Johnson affirms that in his mind:

this case affords one of the most convincing proofs of the continuation of life after death and of the survival of all our faculties that it is possible to obtain. . . .

[Daisy's] artless patter is of infinitely more value—and far nearer the actual truth—than all the learned philosophy and disquisitions of scientists and divines. As Jesus exclaimed, "I thank thee, Father, Lord of the wise and the learned, Thou hast revealed them to the childlike."

In the *Sunday Express* of May 26, 1935, W. Martin of Liverpool, England, wrote of his experience at the age of sixteen when he underwent a near-fatal accident and perceived his "consciousness functioning intelligently apart from the physical body." Today, we would say that the boy had a near-death experience.

"In 1911, at the age of sixteen," Martin began his account, "I was staying about twelve miles away from my own home when a high wall was blown down by a sudden gust of wind as I was passing. A huge stone hit me on top of the head."

Martin then found himself somehow above the scene of the accident, and he could see himself lying on the ground, huddled up, with one corner of the stone resting on his head.

"Quite a number of people were rushing toward me. I watched them move the stone, and someone took off his coat and put it under my head. I heard all of their comments: 'Fetch a doctor.' 'His neck is broken.' 'Skull smashed.' "

Someone in the crowd appeared to know where Martin lived, so a group of men began carrying him toward his place of lodging.

"Now all this time I appeared as though I were disembodied from the form lying on the ground. I was suspended in midair in the center of the group, and I could hear everything that was being said."

As the men began to carry Martin toward his room, he heard someone in the crowd remark what a terrible blow his accident would be to his parents.

"I was immediately conscious of a desire to be with my mother. Instantly I was at home, and Father and Mother were just sitting down to their midday meal. On my entrance, Mother sat bolt upright in her chair and said, 'Bert, something has happened to our boy.' "

Martin's parents began to argue when his father attempted to dismiss his mother's intuitive flash as nonsense.

"Mother refused to be pacified, and she told Father that if she caught the two p.m. train, she could be with me before three.

"She had hardly left the room when there came a knock at the front door. It was a porter from the railway station with a telegram saying that I was badly hurt."

Suddenly Martin was once again transported—

this time seemingly against his wishes. He found himself in a bedroom, where a woman he knew was lying in bed. Two other women were bustling about the room, and a doctor was leaning over the bed.

"Then the doctor had a baby in his hands. At once I had an almost irresistible impulse to press my face through the back of the baby's head so that my face would come out at the same place as the child's."

Martin felt deep sorrow and regret when he heard the doctor sigh and pronounce to the two women in the room, "It looks as though we lost them both."

The teenage boy again felt the urge to take the baby's place, to somehow enter the body as he had done moments before, and to show the doctor that he was wrong.

"But the thought of my own mother crying for me turned my consciousness in her direction—and then straightaway I was in a railway carriage with her and my father."

He was still with them when they arrived at his lodgings and were shown to the room where he had been put to bed.

"Mother sat beside the bed, and I longed to comfort her. After a time the realization came to me that I ought to do the same thing that I had felt impelled to do in the case of the baby. I came to understand that I should climb back into my body on the bed.

"At last I succeeded, and the effort caused the physical me to sit up in bed fully conscious."

His mother tried to make him lie down again, but Martin said that he was all right.

"I remarked how odd it was that she had known something was wrong with me even before the porter had delivered the telegram. Both she and Dad were amazed at my knowledge of her intuitive insight.

"Their astonishment was further increased when I repeated almost word for word some of the conversation that they had had at home and in the train."

Martin also told them that he had been as close to being reborn that day as he had been to dying. He explained that he had somehow been able to observe Mrs. Wilson, who lived close to his parents' home, as she gave birth at the same time that he was out of his body.

"The baby died," he said sadly, "because I would not get into its body. I wanted, instead, to return to my own."

The teenager and his parents subsequently learned that their neighbor, Mrs. Wilson, had died on the same day as he had suffered his accident. She had passed on at 2:05 after delivering a stillborn girl.

Dr. Minot J. Savage presented the following authenticated case for the January 1907 issue of the

Journal of the American Society for Psychical Research:

Two little girls, Jennie and Edith, one eight years of age, the other a little older, were schoolmates and close friends. In June 1889 both were taken ill of diphtheria. At noon on a Wednesday, Jennie died.

In order not to place the additional burden of sorrow on little Edith, both her parents and her physician took particular pains to keep the knowledge of her playmate's death from her.

"To prove that they had succeeded and that Edith did not know of Jennie's death," Dr. Savage stated, "it may be mentioned that on Saturday, June 8, at noon, just as she became conscious of all that was passing about her, she selected two of her photographs to be sent to Jennie."

At the same time, little Edith, who seemed to be aware of her own imminent death, asked those who would deliver the pictures to Jennie also to bid her good-bye.

Edith died at half-past six on the evening of June 8.

"She had roused and bidden her friends goodbye, and was talking of dying persons and seemed to have no fear. She appeared to see one and another of the friends she knew were dead."

Then, suddenly, and with every appearance of surprise, eight-year-old Edith turned to her father and exclaimed, "Why, Papa, I am going to take Jennie with me!

"Papa, Papa! You didn't tell me that Jennie was already here!"

"And immediately," Dr. Savage concluded his account, "she reached out her arms as if in welcome and said, 'Oh, Jennie, I'm so glad you are here.'"

Dr. Savage's story reminds us of an account that Dr. Louisa Rhine repeats in her classic work, *Hidden Channels of the Mind*:

A woman in New York City recounted the 1960 episode in which her three-year-old daughter was denied the tragic information that her seven-year-old playmate, Anne, a diabetic, had died. The little girl was not taken to the funeral and in answer to inquiries regarding Anne's whereabouts, she was simply told that her friend had gone away on a trip.

It was several days after the funeral, when, according to the mother, she sent her daughter to get a particular broom from the hall closet. A few minutes later, she was surprised when the girl returned to her empty-handed.

"Anne won't let me in the closet," she explained to her astonished mother. "She's standing in the hall closet, and she won't let me by."

When the mother became convinced that her daughter was not joking with her or just telling a story, she asked her what Anne was wearing.

"A pretty white dress with a veil," she answered without hesitation. "That's why we can't go outside to play. Anne doesn't have a coat with her."

According to the mother's account, seven-year-old Anne had been buried in her communion dress.

The following day, while she was sitting in the living room, she heard her daughter speaking with someone in the hall. When she inquired, the little girl said that she was talking with Anne.

Trying not to become upset, she went into the hall and asked where Anne was.

"She pointed but said Anne was going out the door."

When she took her daughter to a neighbor's to play, she confided in the woman about the strange incident.

"Together we prayed and sprinkled holy water in the apartment, but I had a very uneasy, sorrowing feeling," she told Dr. Rhine. "Two days later my daughter became ill—and two weeks from the day Anne died, my daughter died of pneumonia."

◆ 17 ◆

Spiritlike Projections to Friends and Relatives

As we have already seen, many children during acute illnesses and suffering have testified to having traveled on other planes of reality. And, incredibly, there also exist the testimonies of hundreds of witnesses who have claimed to have seen the spirit-like image of a friend or a relative appear before them while the living, physical counterpart of the apparition was known to be as many as thousands of miles away.

Stella (Libby) Rife was extremely close to her cousin Bernice Moore. The girls were, in fact, "double cousins." Bernice's father was Stella's mother's brother, and her mother was Stella's father's sister. Since earliest childhood the little girls had been fast companions and confidantes until

Stella's family moved from Lansing to Jackson, Michigan.

Three years later, on a December evening, Stella and a girlfriend were home alone. Stella was about to leave her room and descend the brightly lit stairway when she suddenly froze:

"Standing in the bright illumination stood my cousin Bernice," she stated (*Fate*, February 1968). "She looked terrified. I saw her clearly, yet I knew she could not be there."

Stella ran hurriedly down the stairs, brushing past the apparition and out the front door. She did not stop until she was a block away from the house. Her girlfriend at last caught up with her and attempted to calm her.

Later, when friends stopped by the Libby home, one of the party, a woman who worked for the telephone company, asked if the Libbys were aware that their phone was out of order. Lansing, Michigan, had been trying to call them, and when the message could not get through, the woman said that she would deliver the message personally.

The message was that Bernice Moore had died suddenly that evening.

When sixteen-year-old Darcy Braden's car plunged down an embankment next to a county highway, she spent nearly thirty-six hours lying at the bottom of a ditch, fading in and out of a coma.

Police conducted a massive search for the missing teenager, but no one was able to locate her until her uncle, Fred Anderson, saw her in a dream and told the authorities exactly where she was.

Darcy and her family lived in a heavily wooded area near a small town in the Ozark region of northern Arkansas. She had been elected a cheerleader for the high school athletic teams the previous spring, and in September 1988, with football season going full steam ahead, she had talked her parents, Howard and Mae Braden, into buying her a used car so that she could drive to cheerleading practice and the home games.

On that terrible night in mid-September when Darcy had not returned by one o'clock in the morning, the Bradens were wishing that they had not yielded to their daughter's entreaties regarding her own automobile. There had been rain earlier that evening, and then a dense fog had settled in.

By two o'clock Mae Braden was fearing the worst. Darcy never stayed out late without permission, and she always called if something unforeseen had come up to delay her arrival back home.

Mae Braden's mother's intuition was being activated for a very good reason. The dense fog that shrouded the country roads had made Darcy nervous, and she left her friends almost immediately after the football game had ended. She hadn't even stayed for the after-game dance in the school gym.

The young and inexperienced driver became confused and anxious driving the eerie country roads. She was reaching down to turn on the radio to help her not feel so alone when she misjudged a sharp curve. Inappropriate acceleration sent her car off the road, completely clearing a guard rail and rolling down a steep embankment that was thick with small trees and dense foilage.

Darcy struck her head on the steering wheel several times as the car careened down the embankment. Her seat belt was disengaged, and she was thrown from her car and into a ditch.

First thing the next morning, the Bradens called all of Darcy's friends to see if anyone had a clue to her whereabouts.

"My blood literally froze in my veins when we were told time and time again that Darcy had left early the night before to head straight home," Mrs. Braden said.

After they checked with local hospitals to see if anyone had been admitted after an automobile accident, the Bradens called the county sheriff's department to report their daughter missing.

"Within a few hours the deputies had driven all the possible routes that Darcy could have taken to our farm home," Howard Braden said. "We were now really getting frightened. And although we tried our best to be positive, you know, parents just can't help thinking about awful things like kidnappings, abductions, and even murder. We knew that Darcy was well liked by her classmates and friends, but she was a pretty girl—and we do get some weird sorts of tourist folks up here every now and again."

Darcy lay battered, bruised, and only occasionally conscious near her wrecked automobile. Her clothing had been ripped and torn when she had been thrown into the dense foilage, and her body was covered with cuts.

"Once I saw Cheryl Green, one of my mom's best friends, come walking up to me," Darcy recalled in her report of the incident. "She told me that I looked lonely and she would just sit and keep me company for a time. We talked for quite a while, and then I said, 'Hey, wait, Cheryl, you died three summers ago from stomach cancer. You can't be here talking to me now. I mean, you're dead and all.'"

The image of the woman remained with her, and Darcy became convinced that either she herself was also dead—or she soon would be.

"And then I just seemed to stand up and leave my body," Darcy said. "Pretty soon I was looking down on my bloody and battered corpse, just lying there covered with dirt and broken branches. I just seemed to fly through space. It was neat. I could see the town below me and all the different farms and stuff."

Then, as she passed above the farm of her uncle, Fred Anderson, she suddenly felt herself being pulled downward.

"I heard my aunt Zoe telling Uncle Fred that there was nothing more he could do until he got some rest. She scolded him that if he didn't get some sleep, he might drive in the ditch and that wouldn't help get Darcy back. And then I realized that Uncle Fred had been out looking for me.

"I wanted to hug him and give him a kiss. Fred and Zoe never had any kids of their own, and he had always seemed to treat me so special and loving. My mom said that Fred and I had some kind of special bond.

"Something told me that it was important for me to stick around while he took a nap. I remember turning my head when he shucked down to his underwear and crawled under the covers.

"I just kind of floated around in his room, and when I heard him start to snore, this voice spoke to me. It said, 'You can talk to him now. He can hear you now.'"

Darcy said that she wasted no time informing her uncle exactly where her body lay.

"A few minutes later, old Fred snorted, got out of bed, and yelled to Aunt Zoe: 'I know where Darcy is. She came and told me in a dream. Her car went way down an embankment, and the deputies haven't been able to see it 'cause it's down in a ditch.'"

Darcy watched while Fred rang up her mother and father and told them to get in their cars, and then she felt her Real Self being pulled back to her body.

Mae Braden didn't argue with her older brother. "Fred is as hardheaded as they come. He has never been the least bit mystical. So when he told us that Darcy had just appeared to him in a dream and told him where she lay still alive, we chose not to doubt him for a minute."

When the Andersons and the Bradens met at the revealed curve where the dream had said Darcy went off the road, a few elements of doubt surfaced.

"There were no skid marks, the guard rail was untouched, and we knew that the deputies—and we ourselves—had been by here a dozen times," Howard Braden recalled. "But Fred said, 'Come on, damn it! Darcy told me she's way down there in a ditch.'"

Thankfully for Darcy, her parents and her aunt and uncle managed to keep their faith in her appearance in Fred's unusual dream.

The sixteen-year-old was found just where her spirit image had said the physical representation of Darcy Braden would be lying, desperately needing help.

Mae Braden called 911 from the nearest farm home, and minutes later an ambulance arrived to take Darcy to the local hospital.

For nearly a week her condition was listed as critical. In addition to dozens of bumps, bruises, and scratches, she had sustained a severe concussion, a fractured leg bone, and three broken ribs.

Fred Anderson still does not claim to possess any special psychic abilities. He just knows that he has always thought the world of his niece, and he agrees with his sister Mae that he and the child have always enjoyed some special bond. This time that special love connection and Darcy's out-of-body visit to Fred's dream saved her life.

Although a near-death experience is not specifically mentioned in the next case, we feel that it bears including. In this instance a young boy's precognitive dream of his little brother's death by drowning may actually have prevented a NDE from occurring. On the other hand, the three-year-old in question may indeed have undergone a NDE and not reported it to his parents.

Every night for several months, eight-year-old Jimmy Orlowski of Leonia, New Jersey, was terrified by the same awful nightmare: He saw his little brother Stephen fall into a deep, dark lake and drown.

One can imagine the horror that gripped Jimmy's heart when their parents, Francis and Joanne Orlowski, announced Moose Lake in Maine as the vacation spot for the summer of 1994.

As soon as they arrived, Jimmy did his best to keep his little brother away from the water.

But then came the fateful morning when Jimmy went down to the pier by himself to try to catch the biggest fish in Moose Lake.

Unknown to the solitary fisherman, three-year-old Stephen had followed him down to the lake shore.

The next thing Jimmy knew, he later told the *Examiner*, there was a *splash*. When he looked and saw Stephen's head bobbing out of the water, he "freaked."

There was no way that he would permit the horrifying nightmares of his brother's death by drowning to occur in real life!

Jimmy jumped in the lake and swam as fast as he could to his brother, "who was already sinking."

Then, Jimmy recalled, "I went under, grabbed him around the waist, and lifted him over my head. Then I tried to get to shore."

But the danger was not past. The three-year-old panicked. And as he struggled in his fear, he began to force Jimmy's head under the water.

"I was in trouble," Jimmy said. "I couldn't hold my breath anymore. So I came up and screamed for help."

Alerted to something awry at the lakefront, Francis and Joanne came running and pulled their sons out of the lake.

None the worse for wear after the rescue, Jimmy said that all that mattered was his beloved little brother Stephen's well-being. He knew that his worries—and his nightmares—were now over.

So again we speculate that Jimmy's recurring nightmare appeared to have been a livesaving premonition that may well have prevented *two* children's near-death experiences.

• 18 •

The Healing Ministry of Angels

We first heard of the remarkable case of Paula Williams in the mid-1960s when she was a twenty-three-year-old recent college graduate who had just begun her high school teaching career in a medium-sized city in Indiana. When we met the dynamic young instructor in physical education, who seemed bursting with vitality and a love for life, it was hard to believe that ten years before, when Paula was thirteen, physicians had diagnosed a curious malady afflicting the girl as being caused by an incurable blood disease.

According to Paula, her parents had been told by a doctor who was a devout Roman Catholic that medical science was helpless in such cases. The only thing that he could suggest was that they take her to a religious healing shrine and "pray for a miracle."

Taking the respected doctor at his word, Mr. and Mrs. Williams had begun making arrangements for a flight to Lourdes or some other popular healing shrine.

"But before the journey could be undertaken, my condition worsened, and I was placed in an oxygen tent," Paula said. "It was now up to me to get my miracle on my own."

Rather late one evening, after her parents had both gone to the hospital cafeteria to get some coffee and something to eat, Paula heard a doctor and nurse freely discussing her prognosis.

"They thought that I was either asleep or in some kind of coma, so they were speaking openly and without discretion. I heard the doctor clearly say that it was very doubtful if I would live until morning.

"That was when I really began to pray with every ounce of what little strength of will and purpose that I had left. I asked God for a miracle. And in my thirteen-year-old state of innocence and belief, I expected to receive one."

Paula remembered feeling as if the hospital room was tilting crazily.

"And then it was as if the entire room was spinning wildly. I seemed to leave my bed and just go shooting upward toward the ceiling. And then I saw that *I* was somehow still on the bed, but my consciousness—or what I have now come to think of as the Real Me—was up on the ceiling looking down on the *non-real* or the physical me.

"When I was real little and we celebrated my birthday, Dad would often take a balloon, blow it up and tie the end, and then rub it against his sweater or shirt to build up static electricity. Once he had performed this little ritual, he would stick the balloon up on the ceiling or on the wall way up high where I couldn't reach it. That was how I felt then. Like a balloon stuck on the ceiling of my hospital room."

Paula was confused, then frightened.

Had she died?

If she had died and this was God's idea of a miracle, then it certainly did not coincide with hers.

"My idea of heaven was not being a balloon stuck up on a hospital room ceiling."

Within a blurred period of time that Paula said could have been a minute or an hour, she felt herself moving through the ceiling.

"It actually kind of tickled as I felt myself sort of oozing upward through the construction materials of the ceiling. And then, whoosh! I was somewhere way out in space."

For quite some time there seemed to be nothing but darkness all around her.

"Now I was really getting scared. It was the darkest blackness that I had ever seen or could ever imagine. It was better floating above my body. I cried. I wanted to go back."

Then Paula heard someone calling her name.

"I recognized the voice as that of Grandma Bollinger, who had died about four years before. I couldn't see her, so I called out for her to come and get me."

Suddenly a slim shaft of light pierced the darkness.

"It seemed as though far, far away, I could see an image of my grandmother. She seemed to be beckoning to me, and I could hear her urging me to move toward the little speck of light."

Paula remembered that at this point in the experience she was convinced that she had died.

"I was saddened because of leaving my parents and my friends, but I had always really liked Grandma Bollinger. She had always held me on her lap when we came to visit, and she would make special chocolate chip cookies with marshmallows for me. So I thought that if I would be with Grandma, then death wouldn't be so bad."

As soon as the slightest thought of acceptance of her transition came to her, Paula found that she began to fly toward the light with much greater speed.

"I was nearly at Grandma's side. I could see a small cottage behind her with a beautiful flower garden. Grandma had always loved flowers. And I could smell chocolate chip and marshmallow cookies."

Paula's flight was suddenly blocked by three tall figures in lavender robes.

"I remember that one had a beard, so he was definitely male. I think the others were female, but they could have been androgynous beings. None of them really looked like my thirteen-year-old Sunday school concepts of angels. They looked to me more like people from the time of Jesus and the disciples."

The bearded entity told Paula that she could not join her grandmother on the other side.

"I was upset by this announcement. I thought he meant that I was going to be taken to some other place, that I would be separated from Grandma."

The being explained that what he meant was that it was not yet Paula's time to stay in heaven. He said that she must return to her body.

"I told him that was impossible. I had heard the doctor telling a nurse that I was dying. Besides, I had been sick for so long. I really didn't want to go to that diseased little body."

The bearded angelic figure informed Paula that she would not be returning to the same body. They would heal it before she left their sacred dimension.

"As strange as it seems, it was at that point that all three of the angels opened their mouths and began to sing this most incredibly beautiful song. My entire spiritual essence began to vibrate and to glow. I remember just feeling at one with everything—the angels, God, the universe.

"The next thing I knew, I was opening my eyes

in this oxygen tent. Mom and Dad were standing there with tears in their eyes, and the doctor seemed really surprised. 'She's come back,' he said in a tone of amazement. 'I thought we had lost her, but she's come back!' "

Paula Williams only knows for certain that "something happened" to bring about a miraculous cure of a blood disease that her doctors had decreed was incurable.

"And that is about as technical and scientific as the doctors were able to be: 'Something happened and the disease disappeared.' "

Paula said that for the next four or five years, she was regularly examined by doctors to be certain that her disease was truly "in remission."

"By the time that I was nineteen, they finally pronounced me officially cured. It may have taken the doctors six years to accept the miracle, but I accepted it the instant God gave the angels permission to heal me."

Bernadette Lopez, who is originally from Las Cruces, New Mexico, recalled for us the details of her dramatic healing by angels and her own subsequent rescue of her mother from a fiery death:

"In 1942, when I was just a school child, I contracted some kind of disease like polio that made me burn with fever and left my right leg paralyzed and my left leg painfully twisted. My father or my mother had to carry me back and forth to my bed from the toilet or from other rooms. My mother

was so worried about me that she would sometimes sleep with me in case I needed something
during the night.

"I was very depressed. I was not yet ten years
old, and the doctors had told my parents that I
would probably never walk again."

On Christmas Eve of that year, Bernadette's father had bundled her up so that she could attend
Mass with them.

"We were very poor in those days, and since
most of the little money my parents did manage to
save went for my medicines, there were few presents for my baby sister, Rosa, my parents, or me.
Mother said that the important thing was that we
were together.

"Then, after we had a little to eat, I suddenly began to run a high fever. Perhaps the chilly night air
had affected me adversely or the night had been
filled with too much excitement, but I was soon
shivering and moaning incoherently."

In order to save on their electricity bill, Bernadette's mother would often crawl into bed with
her and read to her by the light of a candle that
she would set on a bedside chair. Although her
husband had warned her of the potential dangers
of such a practice, she felt that the reading of a
special Christmas story would bring some cheer to
their crippled daughter.

"I don't remember at all what Mama was reading. My fever was very high, and I thought that I
was dying. When I entered periods of semicon-

sciousness, I was glad that she was with me. But most of the time I had no idea where I was."

Sometime that night Bernadette was astonished to see two columns of angels appear and stand at the sides of her bed.

"I remember clearly that there were six of the glorious beings on my right side and six on my left.

"And then they began to sing the sweetest, most beautiful song that I had ever heard. And all around them was the most magnificent music being played by an unseen orchestra. I thought to myself, truly this is the song that the shepherds had heard on high on that Christmas Eve so long ago.

"But then they began to sing louder and louder, until their mighty choruses hurt my ears. And the angels themselves appeared to grow larger and larger as they sang louder and louder."

Just as the song of the angels reached a crescendo, Bernadette awakened to the horror of discovering that she and her mother were enveloped in flames.

Bernadette jumped out of bed and dragged her mother from the flames that had engulfed them.

"I pulled my unconscious mother away from the burning bed, and then I began beating out the flames, first with my bare hands, then a bath towel. The bedclothes were badly burned, as well as half the mattress and one of the pillows."

Her father appeared at the door of the bedroom

and emitted a shout of commingled alarm and joy. "Bernadette! You are walking! You are out of bed!"

The miracle of it all had not struck her until her father had shouted it aloud. How could she, a small girl weakened by fever and paralysis, have managed to jump out of bed and pull her mother to safety?

"It could only have been due to the healing energies brought to me by those twelve beautiful angels, who first performed the miracle of healing on my legs—and then kept singing louder and louder until I awakened to save myself and my mother from the fire that had started when she had fallen asleep and knocked over the candle.

"Although mother's dressing gown and nightdress were burned off her body on her left side and my nightgown was scorched black, neither of us had the slightest burn on our flesh.

"But the greatest Christmas miracle of all was that I continued to walk without assistance. My parents never again had to carry me anywhere. Soon I was once again running and skipping rope with my friends, a happy schoolgirl who would never forget the angels from on high and their song of healing. I know that they still watch over me, and from time to time I am aware of their presence."

As we have indicated frequently in the case histories in this book, once children make an angel connection during a NDE, they very often maintain it throughout the course of their adult life.

Dr. P.M.H. Atwater told us of a case from her files in which a young girl continued to search for the people that she had seen while in the Light.

"The girl would go from room to room in her house, searching, looking under the beds, everywhere. She had been traumatized by her particular near-death experience, and she knew that 'the people from the light' would be able to help her.

"Because she was just a small child at the time of her NDE, she had no channel of expression to explain to others what she had experienced. She simply lacked the language and the perspective to tell others of her voyage to the light until she was much older."

Ever since she was a child of five, Janis Ambrosini-Gamble of Clifton, New Jersey, has been aware of angelic observers watching over her. At first she perceived her guardian angel as a glowing ball of light, but when she was about twelve years of age, the entity assumed the form of a man, issuing forth a bright illumination.

When she was eight, the Light Being appeared at her bedside and lowered a dangerously high fever.

"When I was around ten, my guardian angel saved me from drowning. I had been in this leaky old canoe at camp, and when it started to sink, I screamed for help because I couldn't swim—and I had disobeyed the counselors and not worn my life vest.

"I felt my angel grab me around my middle, and I heard him whisper in my ear to be calm, that he would hold me up until the lifeguards got to me."

In the summer of her fifteenth year, while on a vacation trip with her parents, Janis' angel shouted at her to warn her father of a terrible accident around the next bend in the mountain road.

"The sudden panic and urgency in my voice caused my father to pull over to the very narrow side of the road and to ask me what on earth was wrong with me. By the time I explained about my 'awful feeling,' he was mumbling under his breath about nutty females and pulled back onto the road. But when he drove around the bend and saw the horrible three-car accident that we would have plowed right into, he was praising woman's intuition and all the benevolent angels in heaven."

Russell Gamble, Janis' husband-to-be, first saw her guardian angel when they were both seventeen years old and having a picnic in the countryside.

"It suddenly got dark and began to storm, and Russ got really worried because he hadn't yet driven very much and he had borrowed his cousin's car. I told him not to worry. I told him I would pray to my angel to help him drive in the stormy weather.

"Russ wasn't very religious at that time, so he laughed and kind of sneered and asked what good an angel would do on slippery roads. Just then we both saw this glowing figure manifest in the back-seat of the car. A wonderful, calming, peaceful feeling of love and well-being came over both of us, and Russ almost started to cry. He said that he had always wanted to believe in such beings as angels."

· 19 ·

Miracles of Faith and Prayer

When Dale Downey was three days old, the two doctors attending his mother told Corletta and Milton Downey bluntly that their son would not live. The physicians pointed out that the child's heart, liver, and stomach were deformed or subnormal.

Stubbornly, the infant managed to hold on to life. During the first six months of his painful, labored existence, the baby was able to rest only when he would collapse from exhaustion.

Although he amazed the doctors by surviving, life was a continual bout of illness for little Dale Downey.

"I was a sickly child, always taking medicine," Dale told us. "And every time I built up enough strength to the point where the doctors thought that I would be able to survive some more surgery, they would take me to the hospital and operate."

In spite of his doctors' vigilance, when he was fourteen Dale came down with double pneumonia, complicated by heart problems and hepatitis.

"The high fever and the difficult breathing that accompanied the deadly bout of double pneumonia were moving me toward a coma. I could feel myself losing consciousness, and pretty soon I could see nothing but darkness all around me."

Dale had never felt so lost and confused. He had endured little but sickness and surgery in his young life, but he had never felt so alone and so terribly frightened.

"My family made a habit of daily Bible reading and prayer. I had given my life to Jesus three times. Once when I was born and my folks baptized me right away because they thought that I could die. The second time during my church baptism when I was christened. And the third time when I came forward to testify during an evangelistic revival meeting. I surely did not expect to be met by darkness. I wanted to see the holy light."

And then, suddenly, Dale found himself back on the hospital bed, surrounded by his parents, his two sisters, Ruth and Rachael, and his best friend and prayer partner, Milton North.

"I felt so sick, so weak. I told Milt that he would have to pray for me. I was even too weak to pray."

For over an hour Dale felt as though his body

was somehow being passed back and forth between two worlds.

"I would close my eyes in the hospital room and open them in this void of terrible darkness. Or I would close my eyes to keep back the awful blackness, and I would open them back in the hospital room."

When Dale seemed to see Bucky, his long-deceased collie, in the hospital room, his mother thought for certain that the spirit of the faithful old dog had come to take her son home to heaven.

"It was the strangest thing, old Bucky came bounding into the hospital room, just as full of spunk as when he was a pup. When Bucky was alive, I was never strong enough to run and romp with him in the fields and woods, but I thought to myself, 'Dear, Lord, if I am dying, please let me have a good run with Bucky right now.'

"And just like that I seemed to get up out of my dying body with its double pneumonia and all, and my soul started to run after Bucky.

"Bucky ran down the hospital corridor and went right through a wall. I followed him and it was like I passed through some kind of doorway to paradise.

"The sun was bright and shining, and old Bucky was just ahead of me in this beautiful green meadow. There were clover blossoms, butterflies, and all kinds of wildflowers. I remember seeing a little brook running across the meadow and through an apple orchard. I could take deep breaths and smell the lushness of the place.

"And it felt so good to run! For the first time in my life I was able to run. And then I started to laugh, because it wasn't the first time in my *life,* it was in my *death!*"

Even as he told the story forty years later, Dale still believed that it was his laughter that had brought the angels to investigate the disturbance in the tranquil meadow.

"These two beautiful, glowing angels were suddenly just standing there right in front of me, and they wanted to know why I was laughing—so I told them my private joke."

According to Dale, the angels seemed to know all about his life.

"You've had a lot of pain in your life, haven't you, my child?" asked the angel on his left.

Dale nodded, but added that there were people much worse off than he. "Pa always says that as bad as it can get for a fellow, you can be sure that there is someone else who has it a whole lot worse."

The angel on his right asked him if he didn't resent having always been so sickly.

Dale shook his head. "I got two legs, so I can walk. I got both my hands, so I can write. I got eyes, so I can read. I got ears, so I can listen to my sisters play the piano and sing. I have been blessed to know of Jesus and God's goodness, and I got a

mother and father who love me. I don't have it so
bad."

The angels indicated that he should accompany
them to the bank of the slow-moving brook. There,
while he sat petting old Bucky with pent-up affection, Dale was shown a panorama of his life experiences in the smooth surface of the water. He
watched violent moments of convulsions and
wretched bouts of vomiting. He saw the surgeons'
scalpels open him time after time. He beheld himself writhing with terrible fevers.

"It couldn't have lasted very long," Dale said,
"but it somehow seemed like I had watched a
movie of my whole life."

And then the angels both asked him if he wasn't
resentful of such a miserable existence.

Once again Dale assured them that he had
never considered himself to be a miserable person.
"I've smelled new-mown hay, the fields after a
summer rain, and Ma's fresh baked bread. I've
seen my sisters' smiles, and I've heard Pa's laughter
when he reads a joke in *Reader's Digest*. And I've
known the love of family, friends, God, and old
Bucky here."

The angels smiled at him and told him that he
had suffered enough. He would be returning to his
body so that he could be healed and grow up to
conduct a healing ministry of his own. They instructed him that he should be especially mindful
of seeking to help and to heal children.

"You won't be back to see us for quite a little while yet," one of the angels said.

Dale opened his eyes and saw that Reverend McNally had joined the Downey family and friends in the hospital room.

"Everyone there laid hands on me," Dale said, "and each in turn prayed. Immediately I felt my spirit being lifted by the Lord and freed of pain and sickness. I could breathe deeply, my lungs no longer congested.

"An hour later, when the doctor came back into the room on his scheduled rounds, he smiled broadly and said: 'Well, Dale, I can see that you are perspiring and feeling so much better. You look really good, young man.'"

From that day onward Dale Downey was able to lead a normal life. His congenital problems with heart, liver, and stomach improved to stages that they no longer troubled him to any degree of appreciable discomfort or inconvenience. He seemed to have been provided with an abundance of energy, and he has not had any surgeries or serious illnesses in his adult years.

Dale married soon after he graduated from college, and at the age of twenty-six he left high school teaching to heed the angels' commission to establish a full-time ministry of healing. In addition, he wrote and privately published a series of pamphlets on Bible prophecy and healing.

One of his early healings took place in a trailer park near Missoula, Montana.

Dale and his wife, Esther, had been asked to conduct a nondenominational hymn sing that evening and the next three nights that they would remain in the camp. One of the trailers housed a mother and her sixteen-year-old son, who had suffered a paralysis due to sleeping sickness. According to the boy's mother, the lad had not been able to talk or to clothe and feed himself for seven years.

Then, after listening to the singing of the hymns and brief messages from the Downeys, the teenager managed to drag himself to Dale's side.

"I listened to the inner voices of my angels of love and light," Dale said, "and I placed my hands on his head and prayed for God's healing energy to enter his body."

Before the Downeys left the park, the boy was walking and talking normally, and he was able to feed and clothe himself.

Dale has in his files a letter from the grateful mother which informs him that "Michael has done all the driving since we left Boise. It is remarkable how God has given him strength to do that. Oh, how I thank Him with my whole heart, Brother Downey. You ought to see the beautiful woodwork that Michael has done . . . everyone thinks his work is wonderful. And just think! It had been so many years since his hands had been able to do anything. It seems as though it was meant for us to meet you folks."

Once when driving through Chattanooga, Dale

felt compelled to stop and knock at the door of a certain house.

The lady who answered the door was startled by the healer's sudden appearance. Mistaking him for a beggar, she expressed sympathy for his plight, but explained that she was unable to help him because all of her money had been drained by her daughter's confinement in a sanitorium.

Then she leaned forward and whispered that her seventeen-year-old daughter had been sent home to die of tuberculosis. Three years of medical attention had failed to cure her.

Dale startled the woman by saying that it was "wonderful" that her daughter had been sent home. Now maybe the Lord would have a chance to cure her!

Impressed by Dale's manner and confidence and Esther's calm assurance, the woman asked if the Downeys would take a few moments to visit with Norma, if she was awake. The Downeys agreed, and they were quietly ushered into the girl's bedroom.

"I beheld at once her emaciated body, her pale, shrunken cheeks, and I felt the familiar clammy feel of death in the trembling hand Norma offered to me," Dale said. "It was without a doubt the grip of death in the hand that grasped my own.

"I just stood there, holding her hand, permitting the angels of love and light and the Lord to speak through me. I prayed the ministering angels of heaven to send their healing mercies down on this poor girl, and I asked that the angelic beings themselves drive the terrible disease from her lungs. I prayed that she be made whole in the light of the Lord."

Esther stood at her husband's side, softly singing hymns of God's love as he prayed for healing.

"I guess we both lost all consciousness of Earth time," Dale said. "When I truly regained my physical senses, I saw what Norma's mother was saying just couldn't be true. We all saw traces of pink coming into those pale, drawn cheeks!"

Dale looked at the clock on the wall and was shocked to see that they had been in the girl's room for over two hours. He apologized for having taken so much of her time. He hoped that they had not drained her strength or tired her unduly.

"No, please, stay longer." Norma smiled, sitting upright against the pillows propped against the headboard of her bed. "You've made me feel so good. Thank you so much."

Norma's mother asked how she might repay the Downeys for the inspiration they had brought to her daughter.

Dale and Esther insisted that they had no thought of monetary payment, but they asked only that she write them in ten days to two weeks to inform them of Norma's progress.

"Do you really believe that Norma will get well?" she asked as she saw the Downeys to the door.

Dale laughed quietly at the question. "Do you really think that God loves us more than He does

Norma? Do you think that He wants us to be well and Norma to be sick?"

Ten days later, the Downeys received a letter from the woman presenting them with the glad tidings that Norma was up and around.

But that is not the end of the story. Five years later, when Esther and Dale were once again passing through Chattanooga, they stopped to visit a healthy, robust Norma, her fine infant son, and her charming husband.

"The value of spiritual healing cannot be questioned," Dale Downey said. "And it is available to all those who reach out to make contact with God and His healing angels. They healed me when I was just a boy, and I'll happily spend the rest of my life bringing their holy light to other children who need prayers and love as much as they need pills and scalpels."

In spite of current popular interest in such matters as spiritual healing and near-death experiences, most medical doctors and their colleagues, the psychiatrists, remain highly skeptical of any form of nonphysical experience and any claim of success through a method of unconventional healing.

Such an august professional medical organization as the American Medical Association has long recognized the power of faith on the individual mind as a factor that may affect the condition of sick people, and they do not quarrel over the fact that such "miracles" do occur.

In an official statement released many years ago, the A.M.A. freely admitted:

> There are occasional instances in which diseases generally regarded as uniformly fatal reverse themselves without any explainable medical cause, whether or not the patient has had the ministrations of so-called healers.
>
> If such a phenomenon were to occur to an individual under "treatment" by one of these healers, the likelihood is that he or she would take the credit. But the medical profession does not recognize that "faith healing" as such has any accepted merit whereby it can be regarded as having remedial or curative effect in persons who are actually victims of organic disease.

In reference to the A.M.A.'s official pronouncement on unconventional healing, a noted spiritual healer commented to us: "By the same token, let us also then assume that a patient is being treated by a conventional allopathic medical doctor and the aforementioned 'uniformly fatal disease' reverses itself. Would not the orthodox medical practitioner be likely to assume credit for the cure?"

In point of actual fact, all legitimate spiritual healers will give the credit for any cure to God, the Source, All-That-Is, the Great Mystery, or whatever name they may give to their concept of the sacred and the holy.

Despite its powerful and well-organized detractors, serious interest in the topic of spiritual healings has surged in the past thirty years—whether the cures have resulted from near-death experiences, the laying on of hands, or the power of prayer.

Dr. Larry Dossey, former chief of staff at Medical City Dallas Hospital and author of *Healing Words: The Power of Prayer and the Practice of Medicine,* has declared that the power of prayer to heal need "no longer be regarded as just a matter of faith." In his book Dr. Dossey cites more than 130 studies, most of them conducted in the past thirty years, which encompass a wide variety of religions and different prayer styles.

"I have come to regard [prayer] as one of the best-kept secrets in medical science," Dr. Dossey told Leslie Miller of *USA Today.* "When people enter a prayerful state of mind, good things happen to those they pray for."

Writing in *A Doctor Heals by Faith,* British physician Christopher Woodward affirms his belief that "the next great step forward . . . is the realization of the existence of healing powers on the spiritual level which, as yet, have not been understood—though they were seen very clearly when Christ was on earth."

Dr. Paul Tillich was on the staff of Harvard University's School of Divinity when he wrote *The*

New Healing in 1955 and expressed his disapproval of the long neglect of Christ-centered spiritual healing by the world's Christian clergy.

"The gospels, certainly, are not responsible for this disappearance of the power in the picture of Jesus," the respected theologian observed. "They abound in stories of healing; but *we* are responsible ministers, laymen, theologians, who forget that 'Saviour' means 'healer,' he who makes whole and sane what is broken and insane, in body and mind."

An Episcoplian minister who conducts regular healing services told us that it was his belief that "when the spirit, body, and mind are unbalanced, illness follows. With God's help, we can pray and restore the proper balance."

A surgeon who practiced at a major metropolitan hospital admitted his personal philosophy that modern medicine must always be conducted with compassion and hope.

"I often pray throughout the entire time that I am performing surgery," he said. "If a complete healing does not occur, I still consider the prayer answered if the patient is given the strength to be able to live with his or her illness."

Over eighty years ago, Dr. Alexis Carrel, who won the 1912 Nobel Prize in physiology and medicine, stated that he had observed with his own eyes a vicious cancer sore suddenly transformed into a scar. This miracle, he said, occurred after honest, devout prayer by one of his patients.

"Prayer," Dr. Carrel declared, "is the most powerful form of energy known to man."

On Christmas morning, 1993, four-year-old Tyrel McAmmond gave his parents physical proof that God had answered their fervent prayers when he showed the strength necessary to rip open his presents with gusto.

Just a few days before his miraculous recovery from a incurable case of cancer, his sorrowful parents, Darren and Shelly McAmmond, had made funeral arrangements for their beloved son, because the doctors had sent Tyrel home from the hospital, sadly admitting that there was nothing more that they could do for him. The deadly, unmerciful cancer had spread through his body.

In June, Tyrel had been diagnosed with B-cell lymphoma in his liver and abdomen, and for the next five months, he underwent heavy doses of chemotherapy.

At first the exhaustive treatments appeared to be effective, and his doctors agreed that the tumors had shrunk completely. They cheerily informed the McAmmonds that Tyrel could go home with them to Grande Cache, Alberta.

But the cure was not to be so easily won. Within a few weeks Tyrel had suffered a relapse.

When their little boy's temperature reached 105 degrees, the MacAmmonds frantically returned him to the care of the hospital technicians.

The revised diagnosis was not good. The cancer

had spread through Tyrel's liver, spleen, and bone marrow.

On December 12, after an unsuccessful attempt with one more chemotherapy treatment, the despirited physicians announced that the vicious, unyielding disease had beaten them. They somberly advised the MacAmmonds to take their son home and try to make him as comfortable as possible for the little time that he had left.

Darren MacAmmond told journalist Esmond Choueke that he and his wife had "cried their eyes out," but they decided to go ahead with Christmas plans so that little Tyrel would not think anything bad was going to happen to him.

But then Darren and Shelley made a positive decision not to give up. Thy had always been devout churchgoers and firm believers in the boundless mercies of God. And they most certainly believed in the power of prayer.

First they made an appeal to their church friends to pray for Tyrel. And then, spontaneously, a glorious grapevine of love began to spread to others of strong spiritual beliefs, and soon thousands of people across Canada and the United States were praying for the game little boy from Grande Cache.

On Christmas morning the MacAmmonds gave heartfelt thanks to God when they saw that Tyrel was unmistakably getting stronger.

When they brought Tyrel in for tests after the holidays, the doctors were astonished to discover that the impossible had occurred: *The cancer had disappeared from the four-year-old boy's body!*

One of the doctors told the MacAmmonds that only God could have healed their son. There was no medical explanation to account for such a healing.

On February 7, 1994, doctors drew bone marrow from Tyrel's one-year-old sister, Jenae, to perform a transplant to make sure the cancer wouldn't return.

In May 1994 Tyrel remained a picture of perfect health.

Dr. Bowen, head of the transplant unit at Alberta's Children's Hospital where Tyrel was treated, told Esmond Choueke that when the boy had been sent home before Christmas, he was in a "hopeless condition." However, the tests performed on Tyrel a few weeks later showed no evidence of cancer. "The boy was—and still is—in total remission."

While medical science can only record, not explain such impossible cures, the MacAmmonds know that "God looked down on us and worked a miracle—and we'll thank Him every day of our lives."

• 20 •

Heavenly Encounters
with Pets

When she was ten years old, Melanie Ruben-stein was badly burned when she accidentally fell into a campfire while on an outdoor weekend in the Catskills with her parents.

"I remember the pain being simply excruciating," she recalled. "First there was the seemingly endless ride to the nearest hospital with my semi-hysterical mother at the wheel of our van. Dad had burned his hands pulling me out of the campfire and beating out the flames that were burning my clothes and my flesh. I was in and out of my body during that long drive. It hurt too much to stay in for too long, so I elected pretty much to stay 'above it all' in my spirit body."

Melanie told us that she underwent a lot of the

same stages that she has since heard so many of those who have survived a NDE describe.

"I became aware of a long, dimly lighted tunnel, and my spirit self began to enter it. Even as I entered the opening, I could hear my mother's voice as if she were very far away. She was telling me to stay awake, not to die, not to leave them. All her words sounded like she was speaking from an echo chamber."

About the time that her mother parked the car near the entrance to the emergency room of a hospital in a nearby city, Melanie felt her consciousness moving deeper into the tunnel, into an environment of almost total darkness.

"I saw a light, a brilliant light at the end of the tunnel, and I began moving steadily toward it. Just as I was about to reach out and touch it, it disappeared and was immediately replaced by what looked to me like some kind of petting zoo. There were animals everywhere. And then I thought that I must be in animal heaven.

"I walked up to beautiful collie dogs and little poodles, and they seemed pleased when I stopped to pet them. There were horses and cattle and pigs; and I even saw some monkeys. There were lots of birds, like parrots and parakeets and canaries.

"And then I thought that if this was really animal heaven, then my dear old cat Zenobia should be there. She had died just about ten months before. I had had the old tabby since I was two years old. I missed her very much, because I had really loved her.

"I heard a familiar purring sound, and I turned to see Zenobia. I knew that it was my dear old feline friend, but she was glowing as if she were an angel cat. Beautiful, multicolored rays emanated from her body. I remember thinking that I had always believed her to be a very special cat, but, wow, she looked like she must have been the Queen of Cat Heaven."

Melanie reached out to touch her beloved cat, but Zenobia suddenly turned and ran away from her.

"I thought, oh, no, please don't play your silly keep-away game up here in heaven. I was becoming kind of frightened and lonely, and I really needed to hold Zenobia and get some of her love."

Zenobia led her into some kind of maze that had been constructed of interwoven bowers of brightly colored flowers.

"That's when I realized that she was not running away from me. She was leading me somewhere."

After a time Melanie and Zenobia stood before what appeared to be a small cave in the side of a mountain.

"When I looked into the cave, I could see doctors and nurses working over my body. I knew that Zenobia seemed to be telling me that I must return to all that pain on Earth. She rubbed up against my hand and reached out her tongue to lick my fingers. I remember crying out, 'Oh,

Zenobia, I love you,' and then almost as soon as her little pink tongue touched my fingers, I felt my spirit self falling into the cave and shooting back into my physical body."

The next day while she was on her rounds at the hospital, Melanie's doctor asked her who "Zenobia" was.

"She said that I was telling someone named Zenobia that I loved her as I was regaining consciousness from the emergency treatment for my burn injuries. I remember that the doctor just laughed when I told her that I had been brought back from death to life by Zenobia, my angel cat in heaven."

Dr. P.M.H. Atwater told us that she has discovered in her research that it is not uncommon for children undergoing near-death experiences to see animals on the other side.

"I have found it to be fairly common for children to encounter animals, especially the spirits of deceased pets," she said. "I have also found that many children who have experienced near-death phenomena say that they had to go through an animal heaven before they could reach a people heaven.

"Are the appearances of animals symbolical? I can't really answer that. But I do know that these kinds of encounters with animals which are reported in the otherworldly projections of childhood NDE experiencers have not been talked about in the media or written about in books on the subject."

William Serdahely, professor of health sciences at Montana State University Department of Health and Human Development, agrees that many people who have had near-death experiences have met their dearly departed pets as well as their deceased friends and relatives.

Professor Serdahely recalled one case from his experience in which a seven-year-old boy who had been clinically dead for several minutes described floating down a tunnel and being met by the spirit of his dead dog. The boy told the doctors who later examined him that he had awakened in the hospital when his dog had started licking his face.

Carlton Myers told us how his childhood meeting with his deceased terrier Toby on the other side during a NDE had truly restructured his life and put his feet solidly on a spiritual path.

"I was not quite twelve when I got really sick with what the doctors were satisfied to call food poisoning. I found out later that I nearly died, but I was so out of my head that I didn't really know what was happening to me."

Carlton can remember a nurse giving him a shot of some kind, and the next thing he knew, he was floating out of his body "like a runaway balloon."

He has retained a dim memory of some sort of guide just behind him, leading him onward toward a beautiful, wooded countryside.

"I can remember that I was having a conversation with someone or something that I couldn't see, and then I recognized the terrain. It looked exactly like the country around my grandpa's cabin in northern Minnesota. And in the next moment I was sitting on a weathered concrete slab next to the old abandoned sawmill. And Toby, my beloved little black and white rat terrier, was beside me."

Carlton remembered hugging Toby and beginning to weep. Three years before, when Carlton had been nine, the brave little dog had courageously given its life for him when they were attacked by a rabid lynx.

"I knew then that I had died and gone to heaven and that I was being welcomed by my beloved little hero."

And then Carlton discovered that heaven held other blessings for him: Toby and he could communicate telepathically.

Carlton asked the terrier why he had not run from the big cat as soon as they had spotted it. Why had he stayed to try to fight it?

"It was crazy, rabid," Toby replied. "I knew it would come to bite us. I knew that you could not run fast enough to get away from the big cat's angry teeth."

"But we saw the hunter on the hill with his shotgun," Carlton argued. "You remember, the guy on the hill with the .410 who was hunting squirrels. We could have got to him, and you wouldn't have had to stay to try to fight the lynx."

Toby licked Carlton's hands where the tears were falling once again. "You could not outrun the big cat. I stayed to fight."

Carlton's memory became a blur of violent images. He remembered how the lynx had moved toward them, swaying in the crazy-sick dance of an animal afflicted with rabies.

He heard once again the big cat hissing and spitting at them.

He had set out running for help, running as fast as he could for the hunter, making his short little legs pump for all their might up the steep, grassy hill.

He heard Toby's warning growls and snarls, and he was halfway up the hill before he heard the first of the little terrier's terrible yelps of pain.

The hunter did come to shoot the lynx, but he came too late to save Toby, Carlton's dearest friend in all the world.

As if watching a motion picture screen, Carlton saw himself once again cradling Toby's mangled little body, his throat cruelly ripped open, his red life fluid soaking the grass all around him.

"I tried not to yelp and cry, but it hurt too much," Toby explained. "But soon it did not hurt Toby at all."

"But *why* did you stay to fight him?" Carlton still could not understand. "You knew you were too little to fight a big, crazy lynx."

Toby's answer was simple and direct. "Because I love you. I died happy, knowing you were safe."

"But you left me." Carlton wept once again over the memory of his great loss.

"Toby and Carlton are always together in love. All is love."

It was at that point in the experience that Carlton began to feel a peculiar tugging sensation on his spirit body.

"The guide that was somewhere near, but not visible, was speaking to me. He told me that Toby had come into my life to teach me about unselfishness, courage, and love. The voice told me that I must begin to display evidence of greater understanding in my life that I had truly appreciated the kind of sacrifice that another living entity had made for me. I must begin living the kind of life that truly merited the sacrifice of a loving brother Earth creature."

Carlton, who had been careless about shooting small animals and birds with his .22, put away his rifle as soon as he recovered from his illness. As an adult he has been active in conservation and wildlife-protection programs.

"As I grew older and could more clearly evaluate my near-death experience as a child, I could see that my interaction with Toby—both here and on the other side—taught me about the ideal of unconditional love. He also demonstrated the great lesson that there is no death, only a change of worlds."

◆ 21 ◆

Heaven Has Room for Everyone

On one occasion, in order to comfort his disciples, Jesus told them that there was a place for each of them in his heavenly palace. In what some Christian theologians have described as the best-loved chapter in all the Bible, Jesus makes his promise that there exists an eternal home of the spirit.

"Let not your heart be troubled; believe in God, and believe in me also. In my Father's house are many rooms; if it were not so, I would have told you. I go to prepare a place for you." (St. John 14:1–2)

Although we have collected enough case histories of near-death experiences to have derived a kind of general pattern of how the process seems to work (i.e., the sensation of leaving the physical body, of moving down a tunnel, of seeing a bright light, of perceiving angelic beings or spirits of the deceased, etc.), once the experiencer arrives in heaven or on the Other Side, the perceptions of the afterlife seem as varied as the individual percipients. And the words of Jesus continue to comfort us nearly two thousand years later—there is space and variety enough in heaven for everyone.

The great majority of the respondents who have completed our questionnaire of mystical and paranormal experiences are adults who are considering their childhood near-death encounters from the broadened perspective that added years on the Earth plane will bring to a sensitive and philosophical seeker of truth and higher awareness. The following is a kind of synthesis or composite gleaned from the thousands of individuals who have shared with us their memories of heaven and their advent as "children of the light."

Many of those who experienced a NDE as a child now perceive heaven as the summation of perfect harmony and love. The beings that appeared to inhabit this higher domain were described as impressive in appearance; serious yet joyful and happy in behavior; devoted to the concept of spiritual evolution; and sympathetic to the situation in which the youngsters found themselves.

Love seems to be the guiding star, the very energy that sustains the angels, the element that fills the spirits of the departed with unimagined joy.

It was made very clear that all humankind was regarded as one family, and there were no divisions according to racial or ethnic groupings.

Earthly religions or creeds seemed to have no particular meaning on the Other Side.

Most children experiencing near-death have come to believe that when a soul is newly freed from the confines of flesh, it may temporarily be greatly influenced by the belief construct that it held in its Earth life. Numerous respondents stated a similar scenario: Devout Roman Catholics often perceive themselves being welcomed to heaven by a saint or by the Blessed Mother. A practicing Jew may envision Moses or Father Abraham stretching forth a hand of greeting to the next world. A Protestant Christian may expect Jesus or an angel to open the gates of heaven. After a brief period of adjustment, however, once vital matters of creeds and ecclesiasticisms soon fade into matters of no importance.

Although the great majority of the children we surveyed encountered angels and heavenly beings, we have no reports in our files of any of them sighting an angel actually playing a harp. There were numerous accounts of our percipients having heard "heavenly music" and "divine choruses," however.

Certain of our respondents who had a NDE when they were very young, ages two to four, stated that they had believed that they had met and talked with God. At the time they returned their questionnaires, though, they had all revised their cosmology considerably. They now defined God as "entirely beyond all conception and imagination," as "unknowable," as "an all-pervading cosmic intelligence."

Children are not alone in reporting that they found a favorite deceased pet on the other side. Many adults have also testified that they were delighted to have seen a bygone cat or dog in heaven waiting to greet them.

Some researchers have expressed their opinion that the spirits of animals might exist only on the lower astral spheres.

Others have suggested that animals that have been sincerely and deeply loved by their owners may be able to possess their personality characteristics for a longer period of time on the higher spheres.

Although psychical researcher George Lindsay Johnson stressed that his surmise could not be proven, he suggested that animals possessed "a sort of unconscious immortality, which is never cognized or realized in any way by the organism, whether animal or plant," but which "undoubtedly exists and survives." Such a state of survival "is much on a par with energy or force, which, although immortal, is quite unconscious of the fact; and in either case as likely as not returns to the source from which it originally sprang."

Nearly all of our respondents have described trees, flowers, mountains, rivers, seas, meadows, clouds, and the thousand and one forms of nature that we consider to be essential, special, and beloved to us on the Earth plane. In addition, they have witnessed the heavenly existence of houses, furniture, books, clothes, and so forth. Perhaps it is as some have theorized, that everything physical on Earth that humankind has perceived or produced has its mental-spiritual counterpart on the other side.

For many metaphysicians the Next World is a material one composed of some sort of higher matter. Moreover, it is a spatial world that has size, shape, and an environment roughly analogous to our own. In addition, this concept of the Next World also envisions various planes of existence in which the spirit body leaves the physical body at the time of death and advances to another plane, or level, of life. The New Jerusalem would then be a substantially real place with a higher concept of geometry and physics than that which we practice on the Earth plane.

Spiritualist Maurice Barbanell, writing in his book *This Is Spiritualism,* states his belief that it is incorrect to speak of an afterlife or even a spirit world. He maintains that there is only one universe and only one life with an infinite number of manifestations and mergers from one gradation to the next. In Barbanell's view, we are *now* as much in the spirit world as we will ever be.

In the Spiritualist philosophy of the afterlife, the deceased, upon "awakening," will be greeted by those loved ones who have preceded them. Families and friends will be reunited.

Recognition will be no problem, according to Barbanell. "Those who love us in the larger life have constantly watched over us and usually help when it comes to our passing. Because in the spirit world thought is a reality, they are able to show themselves as we knew them."

As a Spiritualist, Barbanell believes that those who have passed into the Beyond live in houses "constructed out of thought, which is the most malleable of substances in a world where thought is a reality. It is as tangible to beings in a spirit world as bricks and mortar are to us."

Barbanell is not alone among metaphysical theorists when he affirms that there is no heaven or hell in the orthodox theological sense. He does, however, perceive them as "real mental states which we have created by the way that we have lived our lives." Life in the spirit, Barbanell states, "is one of continuous progress in which every individual gradually eliminates the dross from his nature in his striving toward perfection."

When asked his concept of the afterlife, Canon Harold Anson of the Church of England said that he believed that the soul would find itself in a world that would be in harmony with its own ideals.

"The real hell," the clergyman said, "will be to

live in a purely carnal world until it becomes a perpetual torment, and the soul realizes its infinite mistakes."

H. H. Price, a former president of the Society for Psychical Research, London, once put forth his view that the whole point of our life on Earth might very well be to provide us with a stockpile of memories out of which to construct an image world at the time of our death.

Such a world, Price hastened to point out, would be a spiritual or psychic world, not a physical one—even though it might seem to be a physical world to those experiencing it. The spiritual-psychic world might, in fact, seem so tangible that the deceased at first might find it difficult to realize that they are dead. By the same token, those who are projecting to such an image world composed of a stockpile of their Earth memories and concepts would also find the spiritual dimension to seem very tangible.

The causal laws that objects in the individual soul's image world would obey would not be those of conventional physics, but laws more like those explored by C. G. Jung. The incoherence of such a dream world of the disembodied would be incoherent only when judged by the inapplicable laws of conventional physics, for the dream objects in the image world would not be physical objects.

Price theorizes that the other world, the afterlife, would be "the manifestation (in image form) of the memories and desires of its inhabitants, including their repressed or unconscious memories and desires. It might be every bit as detailed, as vivid, and as complex as this present perceptible world which we experience now."

Such an image world, Price suggests, might very well contain a vivid and persistent image of the body of the deceased or the one experiencing near-death.

"The surviving personality, according to this conception of survival, is in actual fact an immaterial entity. But if one habitually *thinks* of oneself as embodied (as well one might, at least for a considerable time) an image of one's own body might be as it were the persistent center of one's image world, much as the perceived physical body is the persistent center of one's perceptible world in this present life."

The notion that those experiencing near-death may create a heaven to conform to their individual concepts and images of an afterlife does nothing at all to diminish the spiritual reality of the next world or to deny the reports of those who claim to have been given a preview of the next world during an out-of-body projection at the time of severe physical trauma. Such theories only seek to offer an explanation for the reason why so many different people experiencing near-death have reported so many different kinds of heaven. Their individual perceptions may have been guided to view the ineffable through the "darkened looking glass" of their personal symbolism.

In other words, their near-death experience was

very real but their interpretation of the experience may have been as individual as their unique and personal responses to music, literature, art, love, and the taste of an orange.

We believe through faith and our own personal, spiritual encounters with heavenly beings that angels are very real. But is there a single, definitive description of what an angel looks like? We think not.

Likewise, although the eternally powerful energy source that is our eternal home does most certainly exist, our individual perceptions of heaven may be personalized and, for a time, shaped by our preconceptions of the next world.

The great yogi, Paramahansa Yogananda, founder of the Self-Realization Fellowship and author of the classic work *Autobiography of a Yogi,* held as one of his principal goals the task of revealing "the complete harmony and basic oneness of original Christianity as taught by Jesus Christ and original Yoga as taught by Bhagavan Krishna." In a number of his insights and inspirations, Paramahansa Yogananda disclosed views of the afterlife that appear very much in harmony with the concept of the soul creating an image world of the next dimension.

In the collection of his thoughts entitled *Where There Is Light,* he tells us that our "real self," the soul, is immortal and upon death, the soul goes to God's "astral dream world."

Death is a delusion, the teacher informs us, so we should not pity the person who is passing through such an illusion, for in a little while he will realize that his mortality was only a dream and that now he is truly free and safe.

Paramahansa Yogananda also describes the after-death or near-death experience of "soaring through a tunnel," of sighting a peaceful light.

And then, he states, "the after-death state is variously experienced by different people in accordance with their modes of living while on Earth. Just as different people vary in the duration and depth of their sleep, so do they vary in their experiences after death. The [good person] . . . goes into a deep, unconscious, restful sleep for a short while. He then awakens in some region of life in the astral world: 'In my Father's house are many mansions.'"

On the astral plane that exists for those who love God, Paramahansa Yogananda affirms, "one has the power to materialize anything immediately by sheer thought. The astral body is made of shimmering light. In those realms colors and sounds exist that Earth knows nothing about. It is a beautiful and enjoyable world."

· 22 ·

Hazards of Deliberate Out-of-Body Projections

In her book *Beyond the Light*, Dr. P.M.H. Atwater lists those responses that she has found to be the most common positive reactions reported by those experiencing near-death:

Ecstatic, at the wonder and beauty and glory of [the experience]

Thrilled, because they feel so privileged to have experienced such a miracle

Grateful, that anything so incredible could have happened to them

In awe, possibly unable to speak or to find words

Evangelistic, immediately desirous of telling others

the good news about death and God and the power of love
Humbled, by the magnitude of the incident and what it may portend

Dr. Atwater told us that in her in-field investigations, children go through the same aftereffects as adults. "But to be certain, they do not all come back as beaming little wonder children," she said. "They, too, have light and sound hypersensitivity; they, too, experience bizarre electromagnetic problems.

"But perhaps the biggest problem that children face is, who do they turn to? Who will they get to listen to their incredible experience? They don't have the language to articulate what has occurred to them, and they may be very frightened.

"Parents need to tell the teachers of these kids that they have undergone a near-death experience. If teachers remain unaware of their special problems, kids who have had NDEs are too often sent to the school psychologist or even to a psychiatrist.

"There is a real need right now to address educators and familiarize them with the special needs of the NDE kids. Teachers need to be aware of very important things, such as they should not force a light-sensitive NDE kid outside at recess to play in the bright sunlight."

To balance her investigations, Dr. Atwater has also listed the most common negative reactions:

Angered, for having been revived and forced to leave wherever they were

Guilt-ridden, for not missing or even being concerned about their loved ones

Disappointed, at discovering that they are once again encased in their physical bodies

Horrified, if their experience was frightening

Dumbfounded, if they want to talk but can't or are afraid to

Depressed, at realizing that they must now resume their former lives, that they must find a way to go on with regular living regardless of what happened to them

The Dangers and Hazards of Attempting Out-of-Body Experiences in an Effort to Regain the Glories Experienced While in a Higher Dimension of Being

In this book we have focused upon the near-death experiences of children that have occurred as a result of an accident or illness. We believe that such out-of-body adventures involve a capacity of the human soul that has the ability to contradict known physical laws, but like clairvoyance, telepathy, and precognition, they may be seen as a facet of the nonphysical dimension of our total makeup as human beings. The "natural" exercise of such a spiritual ability is no more injurious to children or adults than the normal exercise of their physical capabilities. As we have seen, those experiencing near-death may be given a sense of well-being and an at-one-ness with the universe beyond that which they have ever before enjoyed. Because of a certain longing for the peace, ecstatic joy, and love with which they were blessed during the NDE, there may be a danger in young children indiscriminately attempting to project their consciousness, their spirits, back to the paradise that they enjoyed during their near-death experience.

Although we believe that it is quite possible to achieve controlled out-of-body "projections" during extremely deep levels of meditation and the employment of certain techniques that bring about controlled altered states of consciousness, we must stress that discipline and discretion must be exercised before any such experimentation may begin. And we certainly do not advise children to attempt such out-of-body adventures solo and unsupervised.

The British scholar and world traveler Dr. Alexander Cannon came to believe in the existence of three "bodies" within the human entity— the physical, the astral, and the etheric. Dr. Cannon held those three bodies to be, respectively, the vehicles of the physical life, the soul, and the spirit. Furthermore, he believed to be fact the claimed ability of certain individuals that they could travel in their astral bodies during experiences other than those brought on by near-death trauma.

Dr. Cannon recommended that spiritual students wishing to manifest conscious and controlled out-of-body projections work steadfastly on first strengthening their willpower before experimenting with astral travel.

In *The Power of Karma* he stated that a strong and positive ego "does not become unbalanced by the invasion of emotion; it builds an astral body which is capable of resisting impulses acting upon it, and deals with joy, fear, and excitement in a discriminating and balanced manner. Such an astral body can only be obtained by disciplining the mind and body and rejecting what is injurious."

Without the resource of a disciplined ego, he sees passive soul travelers open to invasions from the astral plane. The spiritual student who would attempt conscious and deliberate projections must be aware that his or her spirit body may contact forces and influences "which may prove disastrous to its owner."

Arguing for self-discipline and a nobility of purpose, the British researcher states: "The poet who directs his thoughts and aspirations to lofty ideals, the devout worshipper of whatever sect or faith, the soldier whose activities are centered on his conception of duty, the physician devoted to the service of his fellows, will develop an astral body of sufficient stability to resist the wandering hordes of the astral plane."

An acquaintance of ours who claims to be able to slip in and out of his physical body virtually at will admitted to a frightening experience that occurred to him when he was fifteen and shortly after he had begun attempting to practice conscious out-of-body projections:

"During this particular experiment I decided to project myself to my grandparents' home. They were getting up in years, and I liked to look in on them from time to time to assure myself that they were both well.

"I knew that I was truly having a successful projection of my spirit to their home, but then I seemed to sense an aura of malignant evil. I began to feel a strange vibration that I had never before experienced during my earlier attempts at astral projection.

"Looking behind me, I was horrified to see a shapeless black mass that seemed to be swirling toward me. From time to time it would throw itself at the fine cord that attached my astral self to my body, and I discovered that that was when I would feel the strange vibration.

" 'My God!' I thought. 'It's trying to break my spiritual connection to my body!'

"Then in a flash of understanding, I realized that the disgusting black mass wanted to inhabit my physical body. I was filled with a sense of loathing when I considered that a thing of such evil might usurp my fleshly shell. I knew that I had to return to my body at once!

"Telepathically, the thing told me that there was no sense in my struggling against it. It had come to take control of my body. It was stronger than I, so why should I resist it? It argued that existence for me would not be unpleasant in the astral realm. I would be there soon enough after my physical death, anyway. What was a few more years on the Earth plane? Besides, it made very clear, it had use for my physical body.

"I resolved not to be intimidated by the thing. I dived right through it; and although I was momentarily stifled, I was not stopped by the density of its mass.

"Then the race began. The thing seemed to be pacing me, side by side, as I shot back toward my body.

"In an instant I was back in my room, but I was terror-stricken to see that the entity had surrounded my physical body on the bed in a black cloud.

"Each time I attempted to enter my body, I was rebuffed and sent bouncing back.

"I cried out for help, and from somewhere a voice answered me and said, *'You have the power within you to save yourself!'*

"Reassured, I exercised the full force of my will, and I pressed forward into the black cloud.

"I seemed to be surrounded by an inky blackness, and I felt as though I were falling through space—a flaming meteorite hitting the Earth's atmosphere, being turned into glowing dust by friction.

"In the next instant I was back on my bed and opening my eyes. I tearfully thanked God for guiding me safely back to my physical body.

"I felt weak and nauseated. I was ill for three days, and it was at least a year and a half before I again attempted another experiment in astral projection.

"Today, each time before I engage in the projection of my Soul Body, I ask All-That-Is to surround me with white light; and I pray for guidance and protection."

Although Oliver Fox stated that he often practiced conscious out-of-body projections and even provided certain instructions in *Astral Projection: A Record of Out-of-Body Experiences* on how his readers might achieve astral travel, he was also very explicit about the dangers inherent in self-induced OBEs.

In addition to cautioning those with weak hearts and nervous conditions to stay completely away from deliberate out-of-body projections, Fox listed the following possible risks:

Heart failure or insanity, arising from shock
Premature burial
Temporary derangement
Cerebral hemorrhage

Repercussion effects upon the physical body caused by injuries suffered by the astral self
Obsession

Fox himself admitted that this was a formidable list, but he felt justified in presenting it so the neophyte might approach out-of-body experience with a true seriousness of purpose.

It was Fox's personal belief, however, that experiments in astral travel, if practiced seriously and on a high spiritual plane, were no more dangerous than driving an automobile. He also expressed his belief that there existed "unseen intelligences," masters, guides, angelic beings, who stand ready to guide the blundering efforts of those who sincerely seek the divine truth.

The great British seer and clairvoyant, John Pendragon, once told us that he was against "any form of psychic development or any technique that attempts to force the emergence of paranormal talents."

He went on to say that he considered the forced development of spiritual abilities to be analogous to one's picking open a rose bud. One may eventually get the rose open, Pendragon conceded, but what vital element may have been damaged in the process?

"I have no technique to explain," he said. "For me, astral projection just seems to work. Frankly, I don't give a damn how it works!"

A gifted spiritualist medium once told us that

the greatest danger in any kind of out-of-body experience "lies in spirit possession."

Even—or perhaps especially—during the near-death experiences of children, the medium warned, one must be vigilant toward the possibility of "parasites of the soul."

She explained that there are numerous spirits who may be Earth-bound and therefore still desirous of inhabiting a physical body.

"Some feel that they have left too many tasks undone, and they wish another body and another chance to complete their labors on Earth. Unless a spirit has been totally obsessed with such a desire—and such a situation is responsible for a good many hauntings—it can usually be persuaded that it must learn to adjust to life on the spiritual plane.

"But it is the evil entities one must truly be on guard against during an out-of-body experience. These creatures of darkness are always seeking a passive living body to invade. That is why a medium will usually conduct a seance in an attitude of prayerfulness and have hymns sung or a passage from the Bible read. Then, too, we have our spirit guides and angels to protect us from these malignant influences."

We live in a time and in a culture that all too readily dismisses suggestions of evil entities that lurk in the shadows waiting to manifest themselves on unsuspecting men, women, and children. And while perhaps the majority of us believe in a supreme being, in ministering angels, and in a non-physical facet of ourselves that we call our soul, we seem to take accounts of discarnate entities with the proverbially prescribed grain of salt. As we will see in the next chapter, it would sometimes be best to keep that skeptical salt in its shaker—especially when it comes to protecting our children after they have undergone a near-death experience.

◆ 23 ◆

A Blow to His Head
Opened a Door
to the Spirit World

The nightmare began for the Rundquist family when Elaine and her six-year-old son, Jonathan, decided to accompany Jackie Saunders and her six-year-old daughter, Carol, to Lincoln Park. It was the first truly warm day of spring after an unusually dreary Chicago winter, so no one wanted to stay indoors. It was a perfect day to visit the park, Chicago's "front lawn," so to speak, and let the kids run off some pent-up energy.

Little Carol executed a somersault with a bit more bravado than grace, but the two women loudly applauded and cheered her effort.

Naturally, Jonathan would have to thrill the ladies with his own interpretation of the same maneuver.

"Watch me, Mommy!" he cried just before he tumbled his own arms, legs, and tiny torso and overturned on the grass.

As the two mothers once again wildly applauded the acrobatic efforts of one of their offspring, they laughingly gave thanks that they were able to get out of the apartment building that afternoon.

"Can you imagine how the china would have rattled if that thud had been in our living room rather than the park?" Elaine asked rhetorically.

The children ran on, shouting, laughing, and the women sought refuge on a park bench with a good vantage point from which to keep an eye on Carol and Jonathan.

The two neighbors and playmates were racing each other down the sidewalk toward a sandy stretch of Lake Michigan shore when Jonathan suddenly went down.

Elaine jumped to her feet, anxious, concerned.

"Relax, girl," Jackie urged. "He's all right. You can tell he's your first child. Wait'll the next one comes along. You won't be nearly so protective."

But then little Carol was screaming for help. "Mommy! Elaine! Come quick! Jonathan is bleeding!"

Choking back a cry of fear, Elaine rushed to her son. He was lying still, unconscious. He had evidently tripped and brought his head down hard on the cement sidewalk. A thin trickle of blood oozed from his forehead.

Later, at the emergency room of the nearest hospital, the doctor informed Elaine that Jonathan had suffered a slight concussion. "He's conscious now, though. Relax, Mrs. Rundquist. Your son will be fine."

Elaine and Paul Rundquist kept Jonathan as quiet as they could for a week, and he showed none of the signs the doctor had mentioned were possible danger signals. They were greatly relieved that their son seemed to be all right, but they were extremely concerned whether or not they should take the trip that a month earlier they had scheduled for that weekend.

Jackie Saunders urged them to go.

"Listen, you two," she advised them. "After the little shake-up with Jonathan, you could use a little relaxation and a change of scene. Frank and I will take care of Jonathan just as we had originally planned. You know he loves it here with Bill and Carol. We'll promise to keep an extra close eye on him because of his head."

Reluctantly, albeit gratefully, the Rundquists agreed to go away as they had planned.

Three days later, as they brought Jonathan over to the Saunderses, who lived next door to them in their apartment complex, he reminded them to bring him back a surprise.

When the Rundquists returned to Chicago on Sunday night, they brought with them a very nice surprise for their son—one even bigger and nicer than his usual fare because of the special circumstances.

Their surprise was nowhere near as big or as unusual as the surprise that Jonathan had for them—and the circumstances became even more special.

Jackie Saunders gave her husband a "let me handle this" look when the Rundquists arrived at their front door.

Elaine immediately detected the discomfort in her friend's manner. "Is—is it Jonathan?"

Jackie nodded. "It's Jonathan. But it's not what you might be thinking. I mean, well, I think you'd better get him to a doctor as soon as possible."

Elaine felt her knees tremble, and she chewed nervously on her lower lip. She leaned heavily against her husband.

Paul could see that Elaine was doing her best to fight back hysteria. "Good God, Jackie, Frank? What's going on here?"

Frank said that they should see for themselves.

Jackie nodded her agreement. "Jonathan, would you please come here?"

Although Jonathan walked into the room as soon as Jackie called his name, Elaine could see at a glance that something was terribly wrong with her son.

He stared disinterestedly at his parents, then directed his attention to Jackie. "Yes, Mrs. Saunders? You called me?"

"Jonathan." She smiled weakly. "Your parents are here."

Not a spark of recognition shone in his eyes as he glanced briefly at Elaine and Paul Rundquist.

"My parents, you say? These two? I am sorry, but I am quite certain that I don't know them."

The voice that came from their son was polite, a bit stuffy, more like a somewhat cultured man of fifty rather than a little boy of six.

Confused, not really knowing what else to do, Elaine dropped to one knee and thrust a large, stuffed Snoopy dog toward Jonathan. "We brought you the big surprise that we promised you, honey."

Jonathan was amused. "I haven't had anything like that in years, my dear. But whatever should I do with such an object?"

Elaine let the stuffed animal droop in her hands, a look of total shock on her face.

Carefully studying the effect that his aloof rejection of the doll had on her, Jonathan emitted a deep sigh of acquiescence. "Well, here, then. I imagine that this little boy here would like such a doll. No need to stand there so dismally with the thing wilting out of your hands."

Paul and Elaine stared openmouthed at each other, completely at a loss for words.

"Maybe we had better go into the kitchen for a cup of coffee," Jackie quickly suggested.

"I'd rather tea, if you don't mind," requested the voice issuing forth from the six-year-old Jonathan.

"I wondered if you would please continue looking after Carol," Jackie asked him. "Now that her brother has gone to bed, she needs someone with her."

"Be glad to, madam. I have always loved children."

The reply would have been ludicrous coming from a six-year-old boy if all four adults in the room had not realized that something far from ludicrous and quite alien to their normal concept of reality was taking place in front of their astonished eyes.

As they sat huddled around the kitchen table, talking in hushed tones, Jackie explained that Jonathan had begun exhibiting the bizarre behavior almost as soon as the Rundquists had dropped him off at the Saunders' apartment. At first both they and the children had thought that Jonathan was playing some strange sort of game with them, but it soon became obvious that something much more eerie and unusual was occurring.

"It's really weird," Frank commented, shaking his head in wonder. "You know, after the first few hours of his talking in that kind of stuffy manner and acting so differently from the little six-year-old kid I know, I found it difficult to treat him as a child. It's truly as though Jonathan is a totally different person. Last night he discussed business with me! I never expected to find myself discussing mergers with a six-year-old!"

Jackie hastened to interject that Jonathan was not like that all the time. "There are times when he is just fine. I mean, he's the little Jonathan that we all know and love so much. Other times he acts like, well, a rather formal old British gentleman."

The four continued their baffled table talk until Paul turned to his wife and reminded her of the time. "Whatever is going on, we've prevailed on these kind folks and their patience long enough. We'll take Jonathan to the doctor first thing tomorrow. Let's get him and take him home now, so Jackie and Frank can get some sleep. I have a feeling they didn't get too much shut-eye this weekend."

When the Rundquists stepped into Carol's room to collect their son, he let out a small whoop of joy, and his wide smile beamed his happiness.

"Mommy, Daddy, when did you get here?"

He rushed over to them and gave each of them a big hug. "Did you remember to bring me a surprise?"

Elaine felt the secure arm of her husband steadying her. This was all simply too much to begin to comprehend.

Jackie quickly walked over to Carol's dresser and picked up the stuffed animal from the spot where their mysterious "visitor" had left it.

When Jackie handed her the dog, Elaine was hesitant about presenting it to Jonathan.

"Here's . . . your surprise," she said, offering it to her son a bit uncertainly. "Do you like it?"

Jonathan emitted another joyful whoop. "Oh, boy, a Snoopy doll! Gee, thanks, Mom and Dad. Look, Carol! It's just what I wanted."

The next morning Jonathan was scheduled for a complete physical examination with their regular family physician, Dr. Holten. Although the Rundquists did not know their doctor well, they had always perceived that he was an extremely well educated and very broad-minded individual. They would later be exceedingly grateful that Dr. Holten was even more open-minded toward the endless wonder of the universe than they could even have guessed.

Although the examination began with Jonathan, it was not long before Dr. Holten found himself conversing with a very polite British gentleman.

"Extraordinary," the doctor exclaimed after he had chatted with the personality for a few minutes.

Elaine nervously wrung her hands, and Paul asked Dr. Holten if their son could be suffering from some kind of split personality caused by the blow to the head.

Dr. Holten carefully considered the question before he responded. "It seems likely that the severe blow to Jonathan's head was the catalyst that set all this in motion, but this other personality speaks from a frame of reference that is far older and more knowledgeable than a six-year-old boy's."

"But *who* or *what* is it that speaks through my son?" Elaine wanted to know.

Dr. Holten, clearly understanding the mother's concern, said that he would try to ask the personality some pointed questions in an effort to determine more about the alleged British gentleman.

But when Dr. Holten returned his attention to Jonathan, he was dealt a shocking surprise. Jonathan stiffened sharply and the voice and mannerisms changed remarkably. Now, instead of conversing with a small boy or a polite man, he was speaking with a woman who addressed him in a familiar manner.

Paul Rundquist clasped the forearm of the ashen-faced doctor. "What is happening here? How can a woman's voice be coming from our little boy's mouth?"

Dr. Holten shook his head and drew Paul and Elaine aside from Jonathan and the newly arrived communicating entity.

"It—the voice claims to be Mrs. Opal Fenwick, a patient of mine whom I recently treated," Dr. Holten told them. "I don't know what to say. I mean, it sounds just like her. And she's referring to matters that only the real Mrs. Fenwick could possibly know."

Paul crinkled his forehead in disbelief. "But this Mrs. Fenwick. Where is she?"

Dr. Holten lowered his eyes. "She died just a few weeks ago. She died of burns that she suffered in a fire."

Overhearing the doctor's comments, the personality presently inhabiting Jonathan began to speak of the pain that she had endured before she passed away.

Elaine slumped into a chair, mumbling weakly that she felt faint.

Dr. Holten had a nurse bring her a paper cup of cold water, then pulled a chair next to hers and indicated that Paul join them for a conference.

"I cannot find anything wrong with Jonathan physically," he told the Rundquists.

"But mentally?" Paul asked, interrupting the doctor. "He must have multiple personalities or something. Can you recommend a good psychiatrist? We've got to help our son get his own self back."

Dr. Holten shook his head. "We're not talking about some bizarre kind of mental illness here. I cannot vouch for the unidentified British fellow, but that was Mrs. Fenwick's voice and personality speaking through Jonathan."

"Just what are you saying, Doctor?" Elaine asked.

"If it didn't take so long to arrange, I would suggest an exorcism."

"Come on, Doctor!" Paul scowled in disbelief. "For one thing, we're Lutherans, not Catholics. We couldn't even find a pastor who would perform an exorcism. Besides, it's not the Middle Ages, and you're supposed to be a man of science, not some witch doctor who believes in evil spirits!"

"You believe Jonathan is possessed by evil spirits?" Elaine asked incredulously. "This is all getting too much for me to handle."

"I said nothing about *evil* spirits," Dr. Holten

clarified. "But I do believe that Jonathan is being invaded by spirits of the deceased."

Paul got to his feet. "Let's go, Elaine. Get Jonathan. This is the 1960s, not the 1690s. Next he'll be prescribing garlic and wolfbane to wear around Jonathan's neck."

Dr. Holten asked Paul to please be seated. He admitted that much of what he had just said would be considered highly unorthodox by most medical professionals and the great majority of laypersons.

"Very quietly I have, over the past fifteen years or so, developed a strong interest in psychical research, in parapsychology," he explained. "I have been working with a number of other scientists and doctors here in Chicago who believe that man and mind are something other than physical things."

Paul admitted that he believed in the soul. And so did Elaine. But exorcism? Possession? Those, he felt, were very much different matters.

Dr. Holten continued. "We've been conducting rigorous experiments with matters that often appear to contradict known physical laws, and we have examined phenomena—such as that which now afflicts Jonathan—that do not fit into recognized bodies of knowledge."

Elaine stiffened. "Are you dealing with the supernatural?"

Dr. Holten explained that both he and his colleagues firmly believed that these currently unexplainable events would someday be found to fit into the total scheme of nature.

"We recognize that there do exist phenomena that lie beyond the five senses and the reach of the physical sciences. We deal with phenomena in which effect often precedes cause, where mind often influences matter, where individuals communicate over great distances without physical aids—and yes, where it sometimes seems as though the living can communicate with the dead."

Elaine and Paul wanted to know exactly what course of action Dr. Holten was suggesting that they follow in an attempt to solve their incredible dilemma.

"Chicago is blessed with many fine, responsible, ethical mediums," Dr. Holten told them. "I'm giving you the name and address of a woman named Diana Willis, who is one of the best. Please make an appointment with her and ask her to examine Jonathan. I don't really know what else to do."

Elaine Rundquist managed a weak smile. "You are really quite serious about this, aren't you, Dr. Holten? You really think that Jonathan may be possessed."

The doctor shrugged his shoulders as though he were not completely comfortable in his role as spiritual diagnostician. "I believe that it is the only answer that fits all of the symptoms."

That night Paul and Elaine sat around the kitchen table for a long time, discussing Dr. Holten's unexpected advice.

"I never thought I would hear a doctor in the 1960s talking about possessing spirits," Paul said, "but you know, if he's willing to stick his neck out like that, he must really believe that there is something to what he is saying. Hell, I've sat and talked with Jonathan, and I know that I am not always talking to him. I mean, I know my own son."

"Then you're willing to give this Diana Willis a try?" Elaine asked, wanting to be certain of her husband's position on the bizarre matter.

"I guess so. What do we have to lose?"

The next day Elaine called Diana Willis' office and found that the medium was quite busy. It would be two weeks before she could see Jonathan.

In the meantime Jonathan continued to behave erratically. The British gentleman eventually disappeared. The woman who had died from burns, who had manifested in Dr. Holten's office, never communicated again.

But in place of those two entities, several others appeared. Some spoke only once through the channel of the six-year-old Jonathan and were gone for good. Others continued to manifest for quite some time. Before the strange series of occurrences would be over, Jonathan would manifest over forty personalities over a period of six months.

In the two weeks before their appointment with Diana Willis, Elaine and Paul kept a careful record of the individual persons who spoke through their son. They also maintained a record of the happenings and events that the entitles claimed to have witnessed.

The Rundquists noticed that Jonathan's "receiving set" seemed most often to attract those persons who were only recently deceased, especially those who had died in accidents or who had committed suicide.

Many of the spirits claiming to possess the boy had been killed in automobile crashes; and as a consequence Jonathan became terribly frightened of riding in cars.

On many occasions Elaine would become quite chilled by harrowing accounts of fatal crashes that Jonathan would describe as they would be driving over the actual scenes of the accidents.

Another consequence of the violent blow to Jonathan's head was his sudden apparent acquisition of clairvoyant abilities.

One morning the boy ran down the halls of their apartment complex, shouting for help. "They're drowning!" he cried hysterically. "Somebody save them. Their boat is capsizing and they're drowning!"

Elaine managed to quiet him and to ask for further details. Jonathan described four people who had been fishing off the Gulf Coast of Florida in a small boat.

Out of curiosity, Elaine checked the daily newspaper, but she could find no account of such a mishap.

The next day, however, she asked Paul to bring

home a Florida paper, and they were shocked to find a report of the boating accident on the front page.

At last the day of the Rundquists' first appointment with the mediumistic sensitive, Diana Willis, arrived. Later, Elaine would tell Jackie Saunders how impressed they were with the medium's initial reading. She correctly described many of the various spirit entities that had been possessing Jonathan, and she went on to make a number of interesting comments concerning the case.

"This boy received a blow to his head that jarred some things out of place," Diana Willis said upon first seeing Jonathan. "As a consequence, he has become like an open door to the spirit world."

Paul Rundquist wanted to be certain that he understood the medium correctly. "Do you mean to say that our son has become some kind of receiving set for spirits of the dead?"

Diana nodded in confirmation. "Especially for those who have only recently crossed over, those who are confused over their deaths. These troubled spirits see Jonathan as a portal through which they can reenter the physical world. Most of these spirits died violently or in a great deal of pain, and they do not yet understand that they are dead."

The medium's method for dealing with the confused spirits was to place herself in a light trance and urge the possessing entities to come forward. When she could perceive that they had heeded her entreaties, she would converse with them and attempt to help them understand that they had lost their own bodies through physical death and that it was wrong to use the small boy's body to maintain a hold on the Earth plane.

Elaine and Paul were astounded as they listened to the bizarre conversations. Often, after a spirit had been apprised of its condition and the wrong that it was doing to Jonathan, it would express contrition, beg forgiveness, and promise to leave the child at once.

Diana prayed earnestly for the souls of the entities, comforting them and bidding them to go in peace.

At the conclusion of their first session, the medium spoke honestly with Elaine and Paul. "The doorway in Jonathan's head is still open, and I do not know what it will take to close it."

Elaine could not suppress a small cry of distress. "Do you mean that he will always be like this? He . . . we—we will all go crazy!"

Diana shook her head reassuringly. "I have every confidence that it will close naturally in time."

Paul wanted to know how long a time.

"I honestly do not know," Diana repeated. "But until it does close, Jonathan will continue to attract restless spirits."

Elaine reminded her that they had heard some of the spirits agreeing to leave the boy.

"Yes," Diana agreed. "I feel confident that those with whom we talked this evening will not return."

"Thank God," Elaine said, closing her eyes as if in prayer.

"*But*," Diana emphasized, "I cannot guarantee that other new spirits will not slip into Jonathan in their places."

Paul leaned down to place a supportive arm around Elaine's trembling shoulders.

"Each time your son is near the scene of a fatal accident, his mind will act like a magnet, drawing toward him those poor unfortunate entities who hover around the scenes of their deaths, waiting for someone to tell them what to do, waiting for someone to help them toward the Light," Diana explained. "These spirits are lost, lonely, and terribly confused. As I said before, they do not realize that they are dead, and they become very frustrated when they find that they cannot alert anyone to their presence. They seize desperately and thankfully upon the opportunity that Jonathan offers them."

Paul's own shoulders began to sag under the enormity of their dilemma. "What can we do to help our son?"

Diana's eyes misted with tears in empathy. She could feel the anguish of the troubled parents as if it were her own. "You can continue to bring Jonathan to me, and I will continue to assist the spirits on their way to a higher vibratory plane."

Paul lowered his eyes, avoiding the direct gaze of the medium. "We would like to be able to do that, but I'm afraid that we really can't afford to—"

Diana held up her hand to stop him and to erase his discomfort over discussing finances. "My dear people, do not concern yourselves over my fee. I charge people for readings and seances, as that is my profession and my only source of income. Jonathan's case, though, is something different. How can one demand monetary payment for the privilege of setting souls back on the path of their spiritual odyssey to the Creator?"

Elaine smiled warmly at the medium. "Thank you. Thank you so much."

Paul protested that they did not wish to take unfair advantage of her generosity.

The medium clarified her position. "I would be most happy if you continue to bring Jonathan to me, as I would appreciate the opportunity of being able to help these unfortunate souls in whatever way I can. Look upon it as a facet of my ministry."

The Rundquists indicated that they thought they understood her spiritual motivation, and they were grateful for her high moral principles.

"Please understand further," Diana told them, "that you can continue bringing your son to me and I will repeatedly assist the tormented spirits on their way, but at no time will I be able to return Jonathan to you and say that I have cured him. Only time can do that."

The Rundquists continued to take Jonathan to see Diana Willis on a regular basis for the next six months. Each time the boy saw the medium, he had picked up another entourage of lost souls, which she dispatched as best she could.

At last there came the evening when Diana was able to announce to the happy parents that the "door" had closed and little Jonathan would no longer be an unwilling host to possessing spirits.

"You might keep an eye on him, though," Diana advised them. "He has all the makings of a great natural medium!"

• 24 •

Transformed by the Near-Death Experience

When Jewel Elliot Hooker of Clatskanie, Oregon, was seven years old, she died of pneumonia.

As she told the story in the March 1968 issue of *Fate* magazine, early in April 1923 two doctors slipped a door off its hinges in the Elliots' Missouri farm home and used it as a makeshift operating table on which to surgically remove one of Jewel's ribs and part of a lung in an attempt to eliminate the infection.

Jewel's father, Orvie Elliot, had died only three years before, and the child's mother prayed earnestly that she would not have her daughter taken from her as well.

But Jewel overheard one of the doctors telling the other: "No use now. She's gone."

At about the same time, the girl found herself walking across a footbridge into a beautiful place that she thought could only be heaven. At the end of the footbridge stood her father with an angel at his side.

"Go back, Julie May," he said in a gentle voice. "Your mother needs you."

Jewel remembered that she protested her father's behest and said that she would much rather stay with him in that beautiful place.

Childlike, she turned to the angel and said that she would like to see Jesus.

The angel smiled at her innocent request. "Not this time. You have a lot to do yet, and your mother is waiting for you."

Jewel's father urged her to return at once. "Go back now. You can come later. We all will be together later on."

In her account of the near-death experience that she set down forty-five years later, Jewel said that she just seemed to walk back into the room in the Missouri farm home, where the doctors stood over her joyful mother.

"Thank you, God!" Mrs. Elliot was exulting over and over again through her tears. "Thank you, God!"

When she was older, Jewel Hooker said in the conclusion of her account, she learned that she had been dead for fifteen minutes.

* * *

The case cited above, typical of those we are examining in this book of children's near-death experiences, is a solid example of what psychical researchers and parapsychologists have long termed out-of-body experiences—instances in which the spirit, the mind, the soul, the very essence of a human being has been apparently projected outside the physical body to locations across the room or across the country or into another dimension or plane of existence and been able to return with conscious memories of the experience. Spontaneously, in such stress and pain situations as a serious accident or desperate illness that result in near-death, certain individuals have seemingly transcended the boundaries of time and space.

Although we would not dispute the allegations that the greatest number of children who undergo a near-death experience describe remarkable visits to heaven and return to consciousness with amazing accounts of having met deceased relatives or benevolent guardian angels, we must add that our research also reveals a certain percentage who came back feeling so transformed in their inner selves that they felt themselves to be somehow different individuals altogether. In other cases the revived children believed that they had been granted knowledge of who they were in a prior life experience. Still other children have awakened from their NDE with the conviction that they are beings of light from other worlds or dimensions who have assumed physical incarnations on Earth for the express purpose of assisting in the raising of humankind's consciousness.

The matter of formerly sensible children recovering from a terrible accident or a debilitating disease and claiming memories of past lives or alien existences invites extensive speculation.

Are these children, because of increased sensitivity after having survived a near-fatal experience, thereby rejecting an association with Earth or their previous personalities because of all the inadequacies and shortcomings they witness all around them as facets of the human condition?

Does the mental mechanism of believing themselves to be of another time or of an alien world enable them to deal more objectively with the multitude of problems that assail the conscientious and the caring at the dawn of each new day?

But why would such a desire to distance themselves from the harsh realities of existence on the planet manifest at such early ages?

And even in our multimedia age would ordinary children have such concepts as past lives and alien identities fixed in their young psyches as alternate-reality constructs to their normal life on Earth?

Isn't it more logical to suppose that children returning to their parents' arms from death's door would be more likely to be happy to return to life as they knew it—rather than condemn their pre-trauma existence as undesirable compared to a prior or alien life experience?

Perhaps we need to pay closer attention to such claims that issue from children who have undergone a near-death experience.

Frederick Lenz, former professor of philosophy and author of the book *Lifetimes: True Accounts of Reincarnation,* has observed that he has heard several hundred of his regressed clients describing life on other worlds.

Our friend Dr. Edith Fiore, a clinical psychologist and hypnotherapist from Saratoga, California, author of numerous books, including *You Have Been Here Before: A Psychologist Looks at Past Lives,* has stated that a number of her patients have claimed prior life experiences on other planets. What is more, she has been able to use certain data provided by such alleged memories to cure her subjects of health or other kinds of problems.

When one undertakes to explore such phenomena as the near-death experiences of children, one must leave all of his or her dogmas behind. No one knows enough about the incredible reach of the human soul or the omniscient majesty of God to place parameters on either one of them.

If one accepts the eternality of the soul, then reincarnation, past lives, might certainly be one of the forms that immortality assumes in its evolutionary progression toward the Source.

And if one can accept the spiritual concept of past lives, then why must such a return to God, All-That-Is, be traveled only on planet Earth?

If one accepts one God-Intelligence for the universe, why should not each soul experience that divine handiwork wherever it manifests itself?

Furthermore, if one can accept the concept of a progression of lifetimes as opportunities for growth and for learning, why should we be confined to the "classrooms" of planet Earth?

Consider these excerpts culled from the Steiger Questionnaire of Mystical, Paranormal, and UFO Experiences. The various respondents are individuals who, as children, survived a near-death experience and who came back to life feeling changed or transformed in quite unusual ways:

She felt as though she had been left behind on Earth

"I was five, and I had awakened from a tonsillectomy. I remember that even though I could barely speak from the soreness in my throat, I looked around at the people near me in the hospital room and wondered who they were. It took a long time to accept the man and woman who identified themselves as my parents. I seemed to have some awareness that I had been left behind on Earth by my people.

"I can remember many times waking up in the middle of the night and crying that I wanted to go to my real home in the stars. As I matured, I seemed so different from my parents and my two sisters that I always felt that *their* daughter must have died during surgery, and I somehow got dropped into her body."

He feels that he lived with his family as an imposter

"I know my body is of Earth, but I think when I 'died' of polio when I was nine, the soul and mind that I now possess must have arrived from somewhere else. I am now twenty, and I often feel as though I have been living with my family as an imposter. I have often overheard my mother telling people that I became a different person after I nearly died and came back."

His spirit essence originated in another dimension

"I was out of my body, looking down at the doctors and nurses performing surgery on my physical self. I became aware of two luminous beings, basically human in shape, who told me telepathically that I was as they were. They told me that my spirit essence had originated in another dimension and that I would return to my body to live among Earth people to study their ways and to try to better understand them. This was in 1944, long before all the kind of science fiction movies people watch today. I was only fourteen at the time, and that was pretty heady stuff for me. But I have never forgotten the experience."

In adult life Light Beings would incarnate through her

"I had already received the last rites from a priest. I was ten years old, and I knew that I was dying. My parents were at my bedside, and Mom was weeping in deep, sobbing gasps. An angel—or a Light Being I assumed was an angel—appeared beside me, smiled, then took me out of my body. This being told me that I would not die. I would return to life on Earth and grow into a mature woman. Later, the being said, other beings of light would incarnate through me when I would bear children. When I asked the entity, why me? He answered me, because I was one of them."

During an NDE he was shown a Native American past life

"I nearly died when I was six or seven, and I fell out of the back of my dad's pickup truck when he was driving on a bumpy gravel road. I thought I had gone to heaven, because I seemed to be surrounded by clouds. Pretty soon a bright light appeared, and it turned into an American Indian in a brilliant feathered headdress. He showed me scenes of Native American life the way it must have been before the white man came to the shores of this country. I felt that I must have been a member of one of those tribes living in harmony with nature. He told me that my thoughts were true. He said that I would return to my body and that I would help my 'people of the spirit' when I got older. Today, I give all I can afford to help Native American causes."

Viewing an Egyptian past life proved immortality

"I nearly smothered in a freak accident when I was fourteen. I remember feeling like my soul left my body, and then I was standing before the Sphinx in Egypt. I could tell that I was seeing that country as it was in very ancient times. When I returned to my body, I felt that I had been shown scenes from a past life in Egypt, and this experience proved to me that the soul is immortal."

He heard Jesus deliver the Sermon on the Mount

"By the age of thirteen, I had already been expelled from two schools. I was a born troublemaker, and my poor parents were going crazy. And I felt like I was some mutant freak that didn't fit in with anyone. Then came the day when a truck clipped me while I was riding my bike. The three days that I was in a coma, my spiritual essence spent in terrain that I would later be able to identify as quite likely that of the Holy Land. I followed the path of an entity that I understood to be Jesus. He had sandy blond hair, a beard, and a mustache. He wore a long, white caftan-style robe, and he emanated pure, unconditional love.

"I awakened from the coma a truly changed person. Although my parents were agnostics and I had never been in a church before in my life, I became a devout Christian. I will always believe that during my coma I was either able to exist in a time dimension that permitted me to hear Jesus give the Sermon on the Mount—or that I relived a past life in which I had actually been there in the crowd that day to hear him preach it."

• 25 •

A Case Suggestive of a Past-Life Memory

One of the earliest cases suggestive of reincarnation that Brad investigated in the 1960s involved a young girl from a small town in Illinois who had survived a near-death experience after a severe bout with pleurisy.

Martha Bergen was only seven when she had her NDE that cold winter of 1949, and she recalled returning to consciousness in a hospital room and feeling very peculiar.

"It took me quite awhile to recognize my parents and my two older sisters," she said. "I was extremely confused, and I felt as though I were a stranger in a strange, strange land. For at least a couple of hours I simply did not know them or recognize them.

"The doctor told Mom and Dad that my reactions were not all that unusual for a child who had had such a high fever. I can remember feeling as though I were awakening from a dream that I could not quite recall; and then, when I saw their faces streaked with tears, I knew that they had all been praying for my recovery, and my memory of their identities returned."

Bizarre night visions seemed to begin at once. In these powerful dreams, Martha said, she saw herself laughing and moving in a lively manner as she swung her body about in a frenzied dance. She saw herself surrounded by the leaping flames of campfires. She heard the mounting tempo of clapping hands, wild and sensuous music rising to a climax of violent abandon. And always she was dancing, dancing like some unrestrained creature devoted to earthy pleasures.

The paradoxical aspect of Martha's vivid dream was the fact that she was the daughter of a strict Methodist minister, who personally considered any aspect of dancing to be Satan's own jig.

When she was a child of eight, he caught her dancing in front of the radio (a radio was permitted in the strict fundamentalist household only for news programs). The little girl was spanked with the full force of her father's righteous indignation and forbidden to listen to those "infernal disc jockeys" ever again.

At age eleven Martha had not yet learned to leave well enough alone. She came home from school one afternoon, and asked her mother if she might take dancing lessons with two of her girlfriends.

"My horrified mother duly reported my request to Dad, who not only took away my meager pittance of an allowance for two weeks, but forbade me to continue my friendship with the 'dancing daughters of the devil.' "

By the time she was thirteen, Martha had learned that dancing was engaged in only by young ladies who did not value their reputations.

"While my friends were having innocent supervised record parties in the homes of their 'hedonistic parents,' I was sitting at home with a book from my father's approved reading list."

And yet in Martha's dreams she would dance, dance, dance. And how glorious it was!

"My hair was borne on the night wind like the mane of some marvelously spirited mare. I always knew that I was barefoot. I could feel my bare feet strike the smooth ground with a rhythm that made my blood course hotly through my veins. And I would deliberately swirl my skirt and twist it high so that the sight of my flashing ankles and a glimpse of my thighs would provoke the senses of the crowd of cheering men."

Mornings, however, Martha would awaken feeling unclean and wonder why God would send such obscene visions to torment her.

"I often considered confiding in Mom, but I knew that the story of my secret dreams would soon find its way to Dad's ears. I took no pleasure in the prospect that Reverend Bergen might try to beat the devil out of me."

Life for Martha Bergen had settled into a rut of incredible frustration and torment.

"When I was sixteen, in my junior year in high school, I checked some books on psychology out of the library; and I began to theorize that my dream was some kind of wish fulfillment. That is, I may have been dreaming about dancing because my parents did not permit me to go to dances. I further observed that nearly all the girls my age liked to dance, and it was probably natural that I should have been in love with dancing, even as a little seven-year-old girl."

Although the dreams continued unabated, Martha believed that she had found the solution to the repetitive night visions. Never, of course, had she ever considered such a heretical concept as her psyche recalling the memory of a past-life experience.

It was at a New Year's Eve party during her senior year in high school that Martha became more confused than she had ever been concerning the source of the strange, sensual night scene that she had been witnessing since she was seven years old.

Everyone knew that when Martha graduated in May 1960, she would be attending a small church college to become a social worker. Although she was regarded as an exceedingly prim and proper young woman, Martha was lovely and gracious enough never to lack for boyfriends. Of course, many were attracted to her, but few were chosen because Reverend Bergen conducted an extensive screening of the young men who came to court any one of his four daughters.

On this particular New Year's Eve, however, the clergyman had been more intent on preparing the New Year's Day sermon than in examining the moral credentials of Charlie Norris, the young man who had asked Martha to accompany him to a "quiet, well-chaperoned party."

Charlie, who had graduated from high school two years before and was already a college man, had been known to have stretched the truth on more than one occasion and to have swallowed the contents of several bottles of beer or "hard stuff" when the occasion arose. He had also boasted to a number of his buddies that he intended that night to "thaw out" the preacher's pretty daughter.

The party, in short, was not the quiet, sober get-together that Charlie had previewed to Reverend Bergen. It was a noisy, booze-sopping, jam-packed blast!

Martha fought a few moments of panic, but she got a firm grip on Charlie's arm and entered the party determined to have a good time. She was, after all, going on eighteen.

Martha did, however, make Charlie promise not to try to get her to take a drink.

"That was one promise that Charlie actually kept. He did not once tease, cajole, or shame me into taking a drink. He didn't have to. The innocent-appearing fruit punch was laced with enough vodka to quench the thirst of the entire Bolshoi Ballet."

By the time the party goers had assembled to play "Amateur Hour," Martha recalled that she was feeling so uninhibited that she actually laughed at one of Charlie's off-color jokes.

Charlie explained that the playing of Amateur Hour was an old and honored tradition among the young people who had been gathering for New Year's Eve since the parent-chaperoned pop and popcorn parties of junior high school days. According to the rules, each guest at the party must perform for the group when called upon or be subject to the program committee's choosing a prank for him or her to suffer through.

The first performer, Clarise Hutchins, sang "God Bless America" in a high, cracking soprano.

The second contestant earned a solid round of applause for his imitation of their high school principal.

Martha was relieved to note that the critical standards of the audience was being steadily blunted by large doses of alcohol.

"Although I felt a slight repugnance at the sight of all my high school friends and various alumni in varying stages of inebriation, I was grateful that they would probably be in no condition to place high demands upon my performance in the amateur hour. I was grateful, too, that I had my wits about me and that I was in complete control of the situation. Or so I believed when I asked Charlie to bring me another cup of that delicious fruit punch."

By the time that Martha Bergen was called to the floor by the master of ceremonies, there was a wicked sparkle to her eyes.

She was known to have a fine voice in the church choir and in girls' glee club, so a reasonably sober young man had already taken his place at the piano in the expectation that Martha would wish to sing for her entertainment.

She shocked all assembled when she announced that she intended to dance for them.

Most of the young people at the party had known Martha since grade school. They knew well the position of her clergyman father on the evils of dancing.

If they had been shocked by Martha's announcement of her talent exhibition, they were openmouthed and wide-eyed when, after she requested that her accompanist play some "wild gypsy-type music," she put on a demonstration of the most abandoned and exotic dancing that any of them had ever witnessed.

Her long blond hair, which had been worn in a sedate bun piled atop her head, was undone and allowed to flow in sleek ripples down to her shoulders. Her shoes were kicked into a corner, and, barefoot, she executed difficult dance steps with style and grace. She tipped back her head and laughed at the almost hypnotic effect her swirling skirt was having on the men at the party.

On and on she danced—until she collapsed into the arms of a very pale Charlie Norris.

"When I regained my sense of the present," Martha Bergen said, "I refused to believe the things that my friends were saying about me. I remembered nothing after I moved through the crowd to the piano. I recalled that I had intended to ask the accompanist to play something from *The Sound of Music,* as those songs were very popular then. I reached the piano . . . and then I didn't remember anything.

"One of my best girlfriends told me that I had danced like a professional. 'Like a Spanish gypsy,' another had said."

As her friends described the movements of the dance, Martha felt a strange little hollow being clawed away in the pit of her stomach.

"They were all describing my dream, my secret dream! They had seen me as I had been seeing myself in my night visions since I had recovered from pleurisy when I was seven years old."

Martha Bergen told Brad that she had often tried to recapture the grace and skill at dance that she displayed at the New Year's Eve party when she was seventeen.

"Just last year [1967] I did my best to replicate the moves that my friends had described. This time my charitable companions characterized my steps as 'awkward' and 'clumsy.'

"Charlie Norris long ago confessed to having spiked the fruit punch with vodka, but I refused to become intoxicated in an experimental attempt to recreate the wild experience of my dream."

Martha did disclose the fact that she had received an interesting letter from one of her friends who had witnessed her colorful performance that New Year's Eve.

"Janie is a couple of years older than I, and she had been home for Christmas vacation. She happens to be a very talented and agile dancer, and she told me that she had attempted to replicate the dance steps that she had seen me perform. A couple of weeks later, when she had returned to the university, she did her best to execute the steps for one of her instructors, a Spaniard with a great interest in his country's traditional folk music. He told Janie that whoever I was, I had been dancing a very old dance of the *gitana*, the gypsies of Spain, and he wondered where I had ever seen such a dance performed.

"I wrote Janie back and told her to inform her instructor that I had seen the dance performed only in a dream.

"Interestingly, the dreams came less frequently after I had allegedly performed the dance for my friends while in the state of altered consciousness caused by Charlie Norris' spiked punch. Now, seven years later, I hardly ever have the dream."

* * *

Did Martha Bergen's psychology textbooks contain the correct answer to her mysterious recurrent dream when they explained the psychological processes of repression and wish fulfillment?

Or had her dream of assuming the persona of a wildly abandoned "gypsy woman" been a vivid memory of a previous life that had somehow been activated by her near-death experience at the age of seven?

And what about the possibility of possession?

Or even the phenomena that some researchers refer to as a "Walk-In"?

As we keep reminding the reader, there can be no hard and fast dogma when one is attempting to survey the parameters of the soul—for there may be no discernable boundaries at all.

• 26 •

Waking Up as Someone Else

The case of Lurancy Vennum has become a classic in the annals of the paranormal. As early as the 1880s, the circumstances of the extraordinary series of events were triggering debates as researchers attempted to define the mysterious occurence in Watseka, Illinois, as an instance of possession or of some as yet undefined spiritual phenomenon. Today, with the advent of the theory of "Walk-Ins" popularized by author Ruth Montgomery, certain psychical researchers have chosen to label the "Watseka Wonder" as a well-documented early example of a Walk-In. Readers may make their own assessment of this baffling account of a most unusual aftereffect of a child's near-death experience.

It was early in July 1877 that thirteen-year-old Lurancy Vennum told her mother that she had heard voices in her room during the night. The voices had called out her name over and over, and the girl said that she had been able to feel someone's breath on her face.

On July 11, Lurancy began to run a high fever and to have recurring fits, sometimes several a day, sometimes lapsing into unconsciousness. On occasion she became quite violent and had to be restrained. At other times she lay almost corpselike, as if entombed in the ether of some nether world.

The bizarre trances, which afflicted the teenager for well over six months, produced varied effects upon Lurancy. At times she appeared to exhibit obvious signs of pain and agony; on other occasions she seemed to approach ecstasy.

And she startled the conventionally religious members of her family when she said that she had visited heaven, spoken to angels, and established contact with many persons known to be deceased.

Word of Lurancy's peculiar affliction attracted more than passing interest from A. B. Roff, a highly respected citizen in the community of Watseka. His daughter, Mary, had undergone similar fits years earlier and had subsequently died from their ravages upon her young body.

Because of his past tragic experience, Roff sympathized greatly with James and Lurinda Vennum, Lurancy's parents, and he was finally able to persuade them to allow him and an acquaintance, Dr.

E. W. Stevens, to visit the Vennum home to observe their daughter. Dr. Stevens was a Wisconsin physician and a prominent psychical researcher of the day. He was familiar with the strange malady that had beset Roff's daughter, Mary, and hence he was greatly interested in a case bearing such remarkable similarities.

When Roff and Dr. Stevens arrived at the Vennum residence on January 31, 1878, Lurancy was sitting near a stove, apparently in a deep trance.

When Dr. Stevens attempted to speak with her, the voice with which Lurancy answered claimed to be a sixty-three-year-old woman named Katrina Hogan. After a time Katrina seemed to fade into an entity that identified itself as Willie Cunning, a wayward youngster who had died an ignoble death.

Somewhat annoyed by the unproductive task of attempting to sort out Lurancy's constantly changing identities, Dr. Stevens suggested that the spirits who controlled her might select someone of their number who was more rational and intelligent to exercise control over the girl.

The spirits, speaking through the channel of Lurancy Vennum, replied that there were many who would like to assume that role, and the communicating entity named a list of people who had been on the other side for quite some time.

James and Lorinda protested that neither they nor their daughter knew any of the deceased individuals vying to step into Lurancy's body as a controlling personality.

When the eerie roster of souls had been recounted, the voice said, "But there is one whom the angels have chosen—Mary Roff. She will come."

Roff was overcome with excitement when he heard the entity name his daughter as the spirit who would manifest within the girl's body. His beloved Mary had left the Earth plane twelve years before.

"Oh, yes, let her come back to us!" Roff told the spirits.

When Lurancy awoke the next morning, she claimed to be unable to recognize a single member of the Vennum family. She insisted that she was Mary Roff, and she begged Roff, whom she identified as her father, to please take her home.

In spite of Mary-Lurancy's protestations that she did not wish to remain in a house with people who were complete strangers to her, Roff was dissuaded by the Vennums from taking the girl home with him.

The next day Mary Roff's mother and sister visited the Vennum home to see Mary-Lurancy for themselves and to test Mr. Roff's description of the phenomenon against their own witness. Upon seeing her two relatives, the girl embraced them and called her sister by the pet name "Nervie," which only Mary had ever used.

The meeting with her mother and sister seemed

to make the possessing entity even more homesick than before, so a move was agreed upon by the Vennums. On February 11, "Mary" was allowed to move to the Roff home.

During her sojourn with the Roffs the girl was able to recognize every person that she had known while she had been alive from twelve to twenty-five years before. She also recalled during various conversations many incidents that had occurred while she was still alive and in the Mary Roff body.

She never seemed to recognize any member of the Vennum family until after they had made several trips to visit her and the two families had become close friends.

In May 1878, Mary told her mother that Lurancy was coming back for just a bit.

The girl closed her eyes as if being led into a trancelike state, then the spirit transfer took place.

When the Lurancy personality emerged, she looked around the room and became quite agitated by the strange surroundings.

Mrs. Roff tried her best to explain to Lurancy what had occurred since she had last inhabited her body, but the child became very distressed and asked to be taken home to the Vennums.

The transformation lasted for only a few minutes, and the Mary personality was back in the host body.

One of the most interesting incidents in the bizarre dual life of Lurancy-Mary occurred one afternoon when Mary stated that her brother, Frank, should be carefully watched.

"This evening he will become gravely ill," she warned. "He might possibly die if proper attention is not available."

Such a malediction seemed quite strange to the Roffs, because at the time Frank appeared to be quite healthy.

Dr. Stevens checked with the Roff family that night, then proceeded to visit a patient's house in "Old Town." It was expected that the doctor would spend the night there; but for some reason he returned, unannounced, to the Roff neighborhood to stay at a Mrs. Marsh's home.

At about two o'clock Frank went into convulsions.

"Go get Dr. Stevens," cried Lurancy-Mary. "He's at Mrs. Marsh's."

"No," the Roff family argued. "He planned to spend the night in 'Old Town.'"

The girl insisted that the physician was at Mrs. Marsh's, and indeed, that was where he was found.

When Dr. Stevens arrived at the Roff home, he was astonished to find Mary already in the process of treating her brother. And what was even more astonishing, she appeared to be doing everything quite properly—so he allowed her to continue under his guidance.

As time passed, the two female personalities occasionally alternated, the "Mary" dominance receding to allow "Lurancy" to come through faintly. However, the changes were never quite complete enough to obliterate totally the Mary personality or to permit a full manifestation of the Lurancy personality.

Then one day Mary became quite disconsolate. "Lurancy is coming back," she said sadly—and she gave a date and a time.

The Mary personality then immediately set about getting ready to leave, bidding farewell to friends and relatives.

On the prescribed day of departure, Mary and her father, A. B. Roff, were on their way to the Vennum house when the transformation took place. When they arrived at the Vennums, the Lurancy personality had returned, and she was overjoyed at being greeted by all the members of her family. She appeared to have no particular ill effects from her several-month period of spiritual dormancy.

On January 11, 1882, Lurancy Vennum married George Binning, a farmer. The Roff family visited her frequently, both before and after her marriage—and up until the time when she and her husband moved farther west to homestead in 1884.

In a letter to the *Religio-philosophical Journal*, Mr. Roff wrote that for a time after Lurancy's marriage, "Mary" would take control of the body for brief periods and then recede again. Roff stated that the Vennums appeared "afraid to converse with her on the subject lest it should cause a return of the 'spells' . . . and her husband never made himself acquainted with [the phenomenon].

"She never had any occasion for a physician since she left us, never having been sick since then. . . . With the birth of her first child, Lurancy became entranced and did not recover consciousness until after the child was born."

Was the strange case of Lurancy Vennum an example of spirit possession? Or did her fevered visit to heaven set in motion some angelic plan that called for Lurancy's soul to be taken to some higher dimension of being to be rejuvenated while Mary Roff's spirit was allowed to return to "walk in" to Lurancy's physical body in order to complete some spiritual lessons left undone with her own family and friends?

To summarize the case briefly, let us note that Mary Roff had died when Lurancy was only fifteen months old. Although the two families lived in the same town, they were only slightly acquainted. During the period in which the Mary personality inhabited Lurancy's body, she not only displayed the personal characteristics of Mary Roff, but she exhibited a knowledge of Mary's life that would have been quite beyond the capacity of either Lurancy or her parents.

The Roffs themselves were completely convinced that their deceased daughter had returned in the physical body of Lurancy Vennum. One knows how readily eager-to-believe parents might be momentarily deceived in the dim light of a seance room, but the Roffs were able to live with "Mary" for a period of several months. At no time did the personality falter in her knowledge of events and recognition of people with which she would have been familiar as Mary Roff.

At no time did the "Mary" personality claim to be a past life of Lurancy Vennum, for as we have already noted, they were contemporaries for a period of fifteen months. For whatever reason— never, it would appear, clearly addressed by either entity—Mary Roff had temporarily returned in Lurancy Vennum's body, and she spoke always of Lurancy as a separate and distinct personality.

A classic case similar to that of Mary Roff-Lurancy Vennum, in which a separate personality "walked in," controlled, or possessed the body of a child after a near-death experience is that of Iris Farczady, a fifteen-year-old girl in Budapest, who underwent the bizarre experience of sharing her body with a Spanish charwoman.

When well-known psychic investigator Cornelius Tabori arrived for an interview with the family in 1933, Mrs. Farczady informed him that their daughter, Iris, was dead. "She who lives with us now is called Lucia—a woman from Madrid."

Mr. Farczady was a chemical engineer. His wife was the daughter of a distinguished Viennese military officer. Such a respected family as the

Farczadys would seem to have little to gain and much to lose by attempting to perpetrate a hoax.

Mrs. Farczady told Tabori that she had always prided herself on being an enlightened, level-headed woman. Her daughter, Iris, had been a brilliant pupil—an outstanding mathematician and linguist who had studied French and German.

One night in August 1932, Iris had felt ill. Mrs. Farczady had put her to bed and had sat with her.

"Suddenly," her mother said, "she gave a long sigh. Somehow I knew that my darling, clever daughter had died."

She bent over to listen to Iris' heart. It was still beating.

"But I was right," Mrs. Farczady said. "My daughter had died. The person who had taken her body awoke, shouting in some foreign tongue. We tried to calm her, but she did not understand us.

"She jumped from the bed, and tried to run from the house. She kept mentioning Pedro and Madrid. At last we realized that she was speaking Spanish."

Try as the Farczady family did to communicate with the entity, she would speak only Spanish. She could neither understand nor speak a single word of Hungarian, French, or German. It took the concentrated efforts of the large Farczady clan to teach her enough German so that they could converse with the mysterious stranger in their midst.

Tabori addressed the girl in German, greeting her as Iris.

He immediately received an angry protest, because he had not called her by her "real" name.

"My name is Lucia Salvio," she corrected him in her heavily accented German.

During Tabori's interview she explained to the psychic investigator that she had felt very ill that hot August afternoon in Madrid. Her husband, Pedro, had been away at work. When she realized that she was dying, her first concern had been for her fourteen children—one for each year of her married life.

Mrs. Farczady commented to Tabori on the great diversity of temperament between her serious, studious daughter, Iris, and the exuberant Lucia, who sang and danced for them.

"When I first looked into the mirror after coming here, I was shocked," Lucia-Iris told the researcher. "I wondered what had happened to me and where my black eyes and dark hair had gone.

"Now I find it quite pleasing that in my new life, I am such a lovely young girl. My only regret is for my motherless children."

Seeking substantiation for the strange story from a member outside of the immediate family circle, Tabori was referred to Dr. Tibor Huempfner, a Cistercian professor who had spent many years in Madrid.

The professor told him that he had been astonished when the girl spoke Spanish to him and described the churches of Madrid in great detail.

Dr. Heumpfner had also been present at a social event where Iris-Lucia had amazed a Spanish teacher by speaking to him in a perfect Madrid dialect.

• 27 •

Integrating the Soul

Early in 1990 a national publication asked Brad to review the work of a parapsychological researcher at Delhi University in India, who had investigated an astonishing case suggestive of reincarnation in which a small boy claimed to be a murder victim reborn.

When he was only three years old and recovering from a severe illness, the boy began to insist that he should be called by another name, the one by which he was called in a former lifetime. He told his startled mother that he had been a shopkeeper in a town eighteen miles away. He had a wife, two young sons, and he had enjoyed a happy life until his murder was plotted by a rival businessman.

Over the next few years the boy produced amazing evidence to prove his protestations of having lived before as a murder victim in a nearby town.

He showed investigators marks on his skull that were exactly where he said the bullet had entered and exited the head of the slain businessman.

He convinced the woman whom he identified as his wife in his past-life experience by recalling incidents, information, and intimate moments that only her late husband, the deceased businessman, could have known. Interestingly, the boy had been born four months after her husband was killed.

The little boy also made a believer of his past-life father, who came away from their meeting convinced that he had met his dead son reborn.

The boy, who was six years old when Brad reviewed the case, insisted that he had come back to get revenge on the rival who had arranged to have him murdered. He had, in fact, already taken his case to court in his past-life hometown, where he formally accused the local businessman in question of being his murderer.

The six-year-old established such a convincing case that the judge solemnly declared that he believed him. However, the magistrate had ended up throwing the case out of court, because there was no legal precedence of a dead man being able to return to name his murderer.

Had the boy's illness activated a past-life memory that somehow prompted him to believe that he had been reborn with a mission of obtaining justice for a terrible wrong done to him in a prior life experience? Or had the spirit of the revengeful businessman somehow possessed the mind and body of the child when he lay ill and vulnerable to outside forces?

And what do we make of the case of seventeen-year-old Maria Talarico, who was suddenly stricken with a strange malady as she crossed the bridge that spanned the Corace River between Siano and Catanzaro, Italy?

For a time she lay still as if she were dead. Then she began to writhe on the ground as though in awful agony. When she was at last helped to her feet, she was no longer a shy, young schoolgirl. She was the brazen and tough Giuseppe Veraldi.

Three years before, in February 1936, fourteen-year-old Maria and some of her school friends had been crossing that same bridge when they saw a crowd gathered at the railing. Pushing their way through the knot of excited townsfolk, the children looked over the steel bars to behold the battered body of a young man who lay sprawled on the rocks of the riverbank far below.

An old woman from the crowd shook her finger at the teenagers and warned them to take heed from the young man's grim example. "He was a carouser—a no-good! That is how wastrels end their lives!"

That night Maria had heard that the young man's name was Giuseppe Veraldi. He had been found stripped half naked, and his clothes had been scattered about the riverbank. His left arm had been broken and doubled under his chest. The newspapers said that the coroners had determined that he had also sustained a fractured skull. The official verdict declared that Giuseppe had thrown himself off the bridge in despair over an unfortunate love affair.

And now, three years later, on January 5, 1939, Giuseppe "Pepe" Veraldi had somehow returned to speak through Maria Talarico and deny that he had committed suicide.

"That bridge is over a hundred feet high. Do you take me for a fool?" Pepe-Maria stormed at those who had come to investigate the strange complaint that the Talarico family had made concerning their teenage daughter. "I had been drinking and watching my friends play cards at the Gisoso Tavern. I left at midnight with Toto, Damiano, Able, and Rosario. It was those four cowardly scum who beat me and dragged my dead body down to the rocks!"

Mrs. Veraldi was summoned to come to see for herself the girl who claimed to be her son, Pepe.

The entity claiming to be Pepe Veraldi was overjoyed at the sight of her. "Pepe" pulled up a chair for the woman and lavished affection upon her.

"Three years!" Pepe-Maria shouted. "It has been three years since I have seen you."

Mrs. Veraldi had not come without a test for the entity. A brother-in-law who had accompanied her unwrapped a picture of Pepe's sister, whom they were positive Maria Talarico could never have seen.

When "Pepe" was asked to identify the girl, he immediately named "his" sister and went on to relate a humorous incident involving the girl.

Then, beseeching his mother through the person of Maria Talarico, Pepe told her that she must never think that he would commit suicide. "I had been drinking. Twenty-four glasses of wine I had drunk that night. And they put something in my wine. There were four of them. I defended myself as best I could. They beat me with iron bars and stones. They broke my jaw and my arm. My false friends took off my clothes and dragged me down to the rocks."

The entity went on to inform the assembled investigators, which included a number of police officers, that one of his murderers, Abele, had died of a heart attack in September 1938. Toto, according to "Pepe," was badly wounded fighting with Mussolini's army in East Africa. Both statements were later verified as correct.

"Pepe" next astonished the investigators when he told them that the "cur, Damiano," was on his way to the Talarico home at that very moment.

"He has come to make sport of the little girl who thinks she is Pepe, but I am ready for him!"

Within minutes Damiano, one of those whom the spirit of Pepe had accused of murdering him, did indeed appear at the door of the Talarico home. He barged into the house and immediately charged that all those assembled there were as insane as the demented Maria if they believed any of the lies that she had been spreading about him.

The entity retaliated with a barrage of questions about the night of the murder.

Within a few minutes a heavily perspiring Damiano was fleeing from the Talarico home. He pushed his way past the physicians and the police officers, who wished to question him further, and shouted loudly that he wanted no part of such traffic with a spirit from the other side.

During Pepe's possession of Maria, the entity was able to recognize all of the murdered young man's friends and relatives and to recall intimate details about each of them. Some villagers found themselves embarrassed as Pepe-Maria recalled various lovers' liaisons that he had observed.

His memory of his last night alive in a physical body was extremely vivid, and he named everyone whom he had seen in and about the tavern.

Pepe returned Maria to her rightful inhabitation of her body in as bizarre a manner as he had possessed her.

He led the investigators down to the rocks beside the river, stripped off half the girl's clothes, then stretched out the form of an entranced Maria Talarico in precisely the same position as Giuseppe Veraldi's body had been found.

The girl lay on the rocks for about ten minutes before she regained consciousness and began to sit up.

One of the doctors who had followed "Pepe" to the riverbank quickly covered her nakedness with a coat, but the teenage girl was shocked to find herself on the riverbank in such a state of undress.

Maria had not been left with one shred of memory of the two weeks during which the spirit of Pepe Veraldi had possessed her. Shamed by the allegations of her family, the physicians, and the police that she had spent a fortnight claiming to be a dead man, Maria went into seclusion and refused to leave her house for many weeks.

Later, at the request of one of the doctors who had been attending her, Maria issued a statement in which she said that she could remember nothing of what others were telling her had transpired during that bizarre two-week period. She affirmed that she was a healthy seventeen-year-old who had never been ill, and she attested that she had never spoken to Giuseppe Veraldi while he had been alive. She also swore that she had never known him or his family—and that she had never even thought of him or dreamed of him since she had sighted his body on the rocks of the riverbank three years before.

Fortunately, Maria Talarico was in no way mentally impaired by her experience. But she never permitted any of her friends or family members to discuss the eerie two weeks when her body was possessed by a discarnate personality.

* * *

Activation of a past-life memory or possession by discarnate entity on a mission of justice or revenge could well be, according to some psychical researchers, a possible hazard of a near-death experience, especially in the case of children, whose egos and personalities may not be as set as those of adults.

A few years ago in her book *Threshold to Tomorrow,* author Ruth Montgomery popularized a kind of variation on memories of alleged past lives and consensual possession that she called "Walk-Ins." In such instances and in rather unusual circumstances, a particular soul might elect to vacate a physical body and permit another to assume long-term, or even permanent, possession.

In her channeling of the entity "Ascordia" in the April/May/June 1994 issue of *WE: Walk-Ins for Evolution—A Newsletter for Conscious Connection,* Amy Bortner states that there may be many different kinds of Walk-Ins, but the "classic" type is "where two souls agree to exchange their status, so that one soul that is presently within a physical body agrees to leave the physical body, to exchange then, with status, of a soul that doesn't have a physical body so that the soul can take the physical body over. There is an agreement, then, to have a quick and clean exchange of soul energies within the body, and [such exchange usually occurs] when a person . . . is rendered unconscious [during coma, grave illness, an accident, etc.], so that the person is not aware of the soul-energy exchange."

Melissa F. Halsey, channeling Lord Retaliyan, an extraterrestrial intelligence, for *WE* newsletter, assures the "children of the light" that the term *Walk-In* is a simple one "that describes a vast process that is now taking place within many beings on your planet. There are many different individual ways that this phenomenon manifests, according to the agreement between the souls involved, and *yes*, dear ones, there is an *agreement* involved on a soul level and sometimes a conscious level."

Dr. Caron Goode remarks that the Walk-In experience may be viewed in two ways:

"From the intellectual perspective, another soul has walked into you, enabling you to activate new energies and attunements to help you . . . to evolve in consciousness. From the Soul perspective, you activate in some way the potential within the once dormant seed in your inner universe. . . . You allow to awaken within you the memory of who you are in other dimensional forms."

Dr. Goode goes on to state that the planet Earth is unique "in that a vast array of life experiences are available to Souls from several densities. . . . Some exist in material form. Others exist in radiant form. When Souls choose to waken their coding frequencies into one human form or to exchange forms, it first requires a Soul agreement that is binding in the planes of time until the Soul chooses to consciously shift perspective."

In *WE*'s October/November/December 1994 issue, Hannah Beaconsfield writes that she has come to refer to the Walk-In phenomenon as "spirit replacement." That is, she likens it to "the situation you find in a long-running Broadway show, in which the leading actors play out their contracts and are then replaced by other actors. The new actors bring their particular qualities to the parts and there are some changes, but the 'show goes on.' This is, of course, a limited analogy, but it does cast some light on a difficult concept."

And what of the following cases from our files? Past-life memories, possession, or Walk-Ins?

A four-year-old boy in Colorado survived a high fever and appeared normal in every way—except that he now claimed to have been a local businessman who was swindled, then murdered by his partner. The child has caused embarrassing scenes on several occasions when he has entered the retail store and loudly accused the proprietor of having murdered him.

When she was giving birth to her daughter in the hospital, Carla had a vision of her aunt standing near the doctors and nurses. This particular aunt, a favorite of hers, had been drowned in a boating accident and her body never recovered.

After she had recovered from a severe bout of chicken pox when she was two years old, Carla's infant daughter began insisting that she was Aunt Inga. According to Carla, the girl has been able to recognize jewelry and other objects that once belonged to her great-aunt, and she has identified photographs of Aunt Inga's friends in old albums.

When four-year-old Bobby died of meningitis, he told his tearful mother that he would soon be back in her arms. Six months later, the grief-stricken parents feared that they were going to lose their two-year-old daughter, Cindy, to the high fever of chicken pox. When Cindy recovered, however, she no longer seemed to be their little girl. She shunned her toys for Bobby's, and she appeared to be expressing all of her deceased brother's likes and dislikes.

Two days after he had regained consciousness from a violent blow to the head suffered from a fall down the basement stairs, a two-year-old boy told his startled parents in a harsh tone that he hated it when they called him Louis. His name, he insisted, was Albie, and he wanted to go home to his wife and children.

Upon questioning by his father, the boy argued that he was a prosperous farmer who had been murdered by three of his hired men, who had followed him into his barn and beaten him to death with an iron bar.

* * *

Although we are certain that the sort of thing some of us mean when we speak of "walk-ins" has occurred from time to time and has been thoroughly documented in the annals of psychical research, we remain rather skeptical when it comes to the allegations that certain authors and researchers have made suggesting that thousands or even millions of individuals have undergone this soul-exchange process, for it seems to us to violate a number of very basic spiritual laws.

Aware that Brad had often expressed another point of view regarding those individuals who underwent a profound change after a near-death or revelatory experience and thereby felt themselves literally to be "new" people, "Walk-Ins," Liz Nelson, the congenial editor of *WE*, invited him to present his response to the walk-in phenomenon. Agreeing to do so in a "non-intense" manner, presented in the spirit of love rather than discord, Brad began by asserting the same credo of open-mindedness that we have attempted to maintain throughout the course of this book:

> After over forty years of rather rigorous pursuit in the field of the paranormal, I have concluded that no one really knows anything a hundred percent for certain. I have found that most of what anyone believes to be fact is really a matter of taste, opinion, or perspective. Nietzsche said it brilliantly: 'There are no facts, only interpretations.'

"But a number of philosophers, prophets, and teachers of spirit have, over the past ten thousand or so years, arrived at certain general agreements, one of them being that what you sow, you are one day going to reap. There are countless examples in spiritual literature and teachings that one cannot escape this inexorable law. . . .

"If you believe that reincarnation may be one of the expressions that survival of the soul may assume . . . then you may believe as I do that we are living in 'Schoolhouse Earth.' I believe that we chose to put on the fleshly clothes of Earth plane existence in order to learn, to grow, to manifest in a fuller expression of humanhood, and to work toward a 'graduation' to a higher form of consciousness.

"What bothers me most about the walk-in concept—at least as I understand it and the way that I hear most people espousing its doctrine—is that it condones 'cheating' in Schoolhouse Earth. It condones allowing someone else to take the big examination for you because you felt stressed or put upon or weary. Well, such a spiritual proxy may get you through the big exam, but for how long will you be able to fool the Teacher—and will you really ever be ready to graduate?

". . . In my opinion most people who feel that they are Walk-Ins are really manifesting the very ancient and often observed phenomenon of 'putting on the new self' after a revelation or illumination [or *near-death*] experience. Like Saul of Tarsus, the light shines in our eyes and we feel compelled to take on a new name, a new identity.

". . . A new name and a new identity symbolizes for them the profound transformation that has occurred in the center of their being and serves notice to all who knew them that they have become essentially another person.

"In a great deal of spiritual training, individuals, whether nun, monk, priest, or yogi . . . are expected to leave behind their past being, past personality, past problems. Usually they are asked to change their name to Sister Maria Theresa or Brother Mark or whatever—and this has no relation to Gladys Schwartz or Bill Johnson, who were born in Pittsburgh or Wichita Falls.

"When people undergo a revelatory or illumination [or *near-death*] experience, they become less concerned with past prejudices, past conditioning, and many other viewpoints now perceived as irrelevant. When these newly illumined ones see themselves as they really are, they not only send but receive a much clearer signal into the universe. Perhaps, instead of the revelatory [or *near-death*] experience changing individuals, it really allows them to become more their true selves.

"A revelator, an illumined one, [*or a near-death experiencer*] may say to those 'who knew him when': 'Once I was George Anderson, but I was uninformed, unaware [of my true self]. But now something wonderful has happened to me. I have seen the light and found a new inspiration and my new self. I am a new person now, and this is my new name. The words that I share with you are not my own and do not issue from my former self. They come from a Higher Source, and they are channeled through the new person that I have become. . . .'"

Perhaps all of these attempts to articulate and define the ineffable may come down to the desire for each of us to achieve a more profound and meaningful integration with our soul.

The angel Daephrenocles, channeling through Lori Jean Flory, addressed the matter of Soul Integration in the following words:

"Beloved ones, the symphony of light is you. The multifaceted harmonies and perfect balance of Christed vibrations flow freely through your soul. All you need to do is listen and be blessed and inspired by the wondrous beauty of the God Force. Come together, beloved ones, as the grand and magnificent symphony of light that you are and harmonize together through the forces of love and light. . . .

"Recognize, please, that you *are* beings of wondrous light and love, walking the pathway back home to full awareness of the God light within the very cells of the embodiment that you are now blessed to have to experience upon the Earth.

"Know you that there is a long, long waiting list of those who would love to have an embodiment as you do to experience ... Schoolhouse Earth. It is not easy to gain admittance to. Know you just how blessed you are to have this opportunity?

"Love your human beingness; enjoy your human experience. It is not forever on the planet, but the real you—the being of light that you are—*is eternal*!

"All the flames of spiritual light within your soul are to be integrated with your physical being. Know that as above, so below. You are divine, and it is all right to be human ... to feel ... to experience.... Have compassion for your fellow beings—and most important, judge not. Love instead!"

◆ 28 ◆

We Are All Multidimensional Beings

Not all of our Children of the Light received their multidimensional blessings through the metaphysical machinations of a near-death experience. Some received their cosmic contact through more direct and less painful means.

"When I was three years old, the angels and the masters began to attune me for work that we would do together later in life," commented Lori Jean Flory of Colorado. "I had many out-of-body experiences that went on through my childhood, teenage, and young adult years. But none of these experiences brought me near death."

Lori Jean went on to tell us that she had experienced the "tunnel" described by so many near-death survivors, as well as the Light.

"Since childhood on, what usually sparked these experiences were the Masters focusing a beam of light on my 'third-eye' region of my forehead. I have always been able to hear, feel, and sense it; but since I have never had any control over the light, I just learned to flow with it.

"But in none of those instances was I ever near death. I was always fine and healthy.

"I have heard the rushing wind in the tunnel, and I have emerged on the Other Side. I have heard a loud, booming voice shout, *'Go Back!'* just before I crossed the threshold.

"Once before I was returned to my body, I remember looking through a white arbor and seeing grass, gardens, and flowers everywhere. There were lots and lots of roses. On the Other Side, roses emit musical harmonies."

It was just as Lori Jean was about to walk through the arbor that she was swept back to her physical body in a matter of seconds.

On most occasions the laser-like bursts of light from the heavenly beings would strike her third-eye region when she was lying down resting.

"Within my third eye I would see light and letters and words of light. I would also hear celestial sounds. This all seemed to be a gradual process that the angels employed to open things up within me—which is probably why they started attuning me when I was only three. I never really understood what was happening to me all those years, because there was no one to explain it to me. It wasn't until I was twenty-one that I began to comprehend what had been going on.

"As a child I often heard angelic bells and responded to angelic frequencies and vibrations. Some nights the angels would come to attune me three or four times. When I was a child, I did not think this procedure was that much fun, because I was confused by the process and really didn't understand what was happening to me.

"When I was a little older, the Masters apologized to me, saying that they had not intended to upset me, but it was necessary for me to undergo such a series of attunements if we were to work together when I was an adult."

It was in the summer of 1978, between her junior and senior years of college at California Lutheran College in Thousand Oaks, California, that Lori Jean formally learned that her special angelic guide was named Daephrenocles. That was also the summer, while she was working at Yellowstone National Park, that an angelic presence saved her life and helped her to "discover new aspects" of herself.

Lori Jean and a friend had been hiking in the "Grand Canyon" of Yellowstone when she suddenly found herself on a precarious perch on a cliff with a view that was over two hundred feet straight down.

"I knew that if I made one wrong move, I was history. I know that there were angels with hands upon me, helping to steady me. There was really not much for me to hang onto in the way of rocks or bushes. All I could do was to lean forward and use my hands and feet like a spider's.

"It seemed as though that afternoon God and the angels were giving me a choice: 'Are you going to do any more reckless, crazy things that you know you should not be doing? Or are you going to concentrate more upon spiritual growth in your life?'

"It really did seem like I was standing at a crossroads in my life, because in so many ways I did feel unhappy and insecure. And at the same time I was also receiving an emotional, mental, and spiritual healing from the angels and from God."

After what seemed an eternity of taking little "ant's footsteps," Lori Jean did reach the top of the canyon, where pine trees, grass, and much firmer footing awaited her. Her friend was able to reach down and pull her up to solid ground.

"I felt so weak, I was certain that I was going to faint. No one can imagine the relief and the drained emotions that I felt.

"And I *knew* that I would never do such a thing again. I knew at that moment the answer to my crossroads question. I would *definitely* concentrate more upon my spiritual growth. I *knew* that there had been an invisible presence all around me that had helped to keep me from falling as I made my way out of that canyon. To say that I would be grateful to God and the angels forever would be an understatement. My rescue and my spiritual healing was life transforming for me."

Now thirty-seven, Lori Jean and her husband, Charles, publish a newsletter of angelic messages and conduct special counseling sessions for those seeking information about the heavenly realms. The following angelic comments and observations were received by Lori Jean and are reprinted here with her permission.

As you awaken to the grandeur within you, we shall empower you. When you have awakened fully to our presence, we are also fully empowered to assist you in your growth. . . . Truly, you are clothed in the skin and bone of physicality. But we have come to tell you that you are so much more than this. You are light; you are divine; you are Beings of Light.

Forever do we watch over you, for never are you alone: We are one. An angel's love is the reflection of your heart. An angel's love creates the perfect space to see your true self within the heart.

Truly do each of you have your own unique music of the soul that to us of the Light, who love you, is audible. Truly, we are mirrors of you, here to awaken you gently to who you really are: You are beings of light, pure love, wisdom, and truth. We have come to remind you of your divinity, of the beauty that you are. The more you love, grow, share, care, and help others, the brighter your auric beacon becomes; and the more noticeable you become to us who love you.

Allow the healing vibrations of angelic music to enfold and encompass you. Allow your wondrous selves to be lifted and filled through the heart.

We are here to love you and to help you. Blessed ones, we are partners of light. You are each an instrument for God's light. You are in partnership with the light.

Many paths lead to the light of God—none better or lesser than another.

We have a relationship of working with you, as partners in God's Light to assist you in seeing the incredible soul beauty of your own being. We come to teach you to love, to have compassion, to help one another as we are helping you. There is a celebration of joy within the angelic kingdoms every time an expression of love radiates from the heart of one of you. We ask you to value one another, to love one another, to respect and have faith in one another.

Reach for the Light, beloved ones. We are right here lifting you up!

From the Steiger Questionnaire of Mystical, Paranormal, and UFO Experiences:

Dr. G.H., a clinical and child psychologist from Texas, stated: "I saw my first angel at about age six. I have spoken with many so-called deceased entities. I had one experience with a blinding white light, many clairvoyant and precognitive events."

"At age five," according to *S.S.*, a psychotherapist from New York, "an ethereal female figure appeared at the foot of my bed. This entity frightened me into leaving the room. There were gunshots outside the house that ricocheted into my bed. Had I remained there, I would have been killed.

"I now regularly make contact with this entity through meditation, but she has also appeared spontaneously. I can also hear her. She guides me, scolds me, corrects me. Recently, I have felt her massage my face and neck when I get tired. She sometimes appears as a very bright light in my room."

R.G., a businessman from Missouri, has retained very clear impressions of himself as a child around the age of four admiring with wonder and delight a white, vibrant sphere of light that had materialized near him. He has also recalled the presence of four entities observing him as he discovered the glowing ball of light.

"From my understanding now, I perceive that these entities were from a dimension that is of a vibration that is much higher than ours, but not as

high as the level of Soul. They have since explained to me that their place of origin exists in a
dimension somewhere between our earthly vibration and Soul vibration."

Illiana from Massachusetts, who defines herself
as a "Channel of Light," told us that at twelve and
a half, she received a profound inner experience:

"At this time my parents and I were attending
some religious lectures. We had been Roman
Catholics, and we were considering some changes.

"One night, following a very fine lecture, I came
out of the auditorium feeling so good, so different
from any other time. Perhaps to say that an Inner
Being had entered my body and had poured light
beams in every cell of my body would give some
idea of the feeling I had. I felt warm, loving, totally
delightful, and *free*.

"The same thing happened to my father. In fact,
it was he who first spoke of how he felt. We were
both so exhilarated. From that day forward, Dad
was able to read—something he could not do prior
to this experience, because he had been deprived
of an education.

"As for myself, until that time I had had a mono-
tone singing voice. I could not carry a tune. From
that night onward, I had a singing gift bestowed
upon me that I have used ever since to provide
consciousness raising music. Also, from that night
onward, I dedicated my life to working for God."

The first messages that she received, Illiana

said, were "heard" through telepathic communication.

"Since that time I always receive contact from the Messengers of Light through a telepathic 'sensing' of the messages. Then, after a period of deep silence and meditation, I write down the impressions on paper.

"The messages are always of a high spiritual nature. Never do I receive the kind of psychic impressions which some others do—nor do I seek them. I prefer to be a Channel of Light, revealing truths that must be disclosed to humankind in these changing times."

On one point concerning the near-death experiences of children, all our experts are in total agreement: *They are going to increase.*

Why?

Well, here we have agreement on one basic reason and differing interpretations of the other.

Everyone agrees that accounts of near-death experiences will increase because of advances in medical science and technology. Literally, more children and adults will be pulled back from the other side due to dedicated doctors who won't let go of the "silver cord" that they have anchored to their increased proficiency in saving lives that previously would have been lost.

A lesser reason why knowledge of NDEs is increasing must be attributed to the remarkable new technologies of the electronic media. Topics such as near-death experiences, which were once limited to arcane reference works and metaphysical study groups, are now the delight of television talk shows and are broadcast instantaneously for millions to view simultaneously.

Nearly everyone agrees that the other basic reason why near-death experiences will increase is because of a general process of evolution that the human species is currently undergoing. Some see this next evolutionary step as one our species will attain through greater heights of adaptability to a dramatically changing environment. Others, such as John White, see the working out of a greater cosmic plan for humankind.

"There is a blueprint upon which human destiny is being acted out," he told us. "There are stages in the growth of the human species that are marked by an acceleration in the evolution of consciousness."

As we learned in Chapter 5, White considers a near-death experience to be a "crash course in spirituality," but he adds that it is at a low level in the hierarchy of trans-personal states of awareness.

"The NDE is considered the first initiation in the mystery schools," he pointed out. "While the NDE is enlightening, it is not enlightenment itself."

In his opinion, the Beings of Light so often reported in accounts of near-death experiences are entities from a more advanced state of evolution, a state toward which we human beings are progressing.

"I foresee for the human species an evolutionary level that the Light Beings presently exhibit," he said. "It is a state of consciousness marked by unity. These beings—Ascended Masters, to use another term—show us such unconditional love because they've been through it all before. They have trod the path before us, they've worn bodies of flesh, and they know all that the human drama encompasses."

John White has given the name *Homo Noeticus* to the evolving form of humanity that he envisions:

"Their changed psychology is based on expression, not suppression, of feeling.

"Their motivation is cooperative and loving, not competitive and aggressive.

"Their sense of logic is multilevel, integrated, simultaneous; it is not linear, sequential, either-or.

"Their identity is sharing-collective, not isolated-individual.

"Their psychic abilities are used for benevolent and ethical purposes, not harmful and immoral ones.

"The conventional ways of society do not satisfy them. The search for new ways of living concerns them."

John White is by no means alone when he foresees an major step in our species evolution. Such scientists as physicist Dr. William Tiller have asserted that our species appears to be undergoing a biological transformation that is presently occuring so widely in the human family as to appear to be mutational. Others predict that humankind may be standing on the precipice of a great leap forward in both its physical and spiritual evolution.

The current interest in such illumination and individual mystical experiences as the NDE will not fade away, for our children are paying close attention to such accounts. Vicariously, through the dramatic spiritual encounters of thousands of testifiers, they are being told the great truth that we are all multidimensional beings. Each of us possesses a temporal, physical body and an eternal soul body. And this marvelous soul body can exist simultaneously on many levels of consciousness and can travel unimpeded to higher dimensions of reality.

Sri Aurobindo writes in the *Life Divine* that in our "externalized surface existence," it is the world that seems to create us. But in the expression of spirit "it is we who must create ourselves and our world. In this new formula of creation, the inner life becomes the first importance, and the rest can be only its expression and outcome. It is this, indeed, that is indicated by our own strivings toward . . . perfection of our own soul and mind and life and the perfection of the life of the race."

With the knowledge that we are all multidimensional beings comes the awareness that our Soul is both universal and individual and that we have the ability to be elevated to higher realms of consciousness and spiritual communion.

We know that we have the ability to tap into an eternal transmission of universal truths from which we may draw power and inspiration.

We know that we have the ability to become one with the Source of All-That-Is and to evolve as spiritual beings.

This knowledge is the legacy that we bequeath to all future generations of Children of the Light.

HEARTWARMING STORIES

☐ **EDGAR ALLAN by John Neufeld.** In this penetrating novel, John Neufeld examines the problems that arise when a white middle class
family adopts a black child.   (167759—$3.99)

☐ **LISA, BRIGHT AND DARK by John Neufeld.** Lisa is slowly going mad
but her symptoms, even an attempted suicide, fail to alert her
parents or teachers to her illness. She finds compassion only from
three girlfriends who band together to provide what they call "group
therapy."   (166841—$3.99)

☐ **THEY CAGE THE ANIMALS AT NIGHT by Jennings Michael Burch.** A
heart-wrenching autobiographical account of a child's oddysey
through foster homes, orphanages, and institutions. He was a little
boy who finally triumphed over loneliness to find the courage to
reach out for love—and found it waiting for him.(159411—$4.99)

Prices slightly higher in Canada